WILLIAM SHAKESPEARE
KING LEAR

Illustrated by Ian Pollock

OVAL PROJECTS LIMITED

SIDGWICK & JACKSON LIMITED

Published by Oval Projects Limited
335 Kennington Road, London SE11 4QE

British Library Cataloguing in Publication Data
Shakespeare, William
    King Lear. – (Oval Cartoon Shakespeare)
    1. Shakespeare, William, King Lear –
    Pictorial works
    I. Title   II. Gibson, David
    III. Pollock, Ian
    822.3'3   PR2823

ISBN O 283 99064 3 hardcover
ISBN O 283 99077 5 softcover

Edited by David Gibson, London
Series design by Jim Wire, Charing, Kent
Lettering by June Sinclair, Tunbridge Wells, Kent

Origination by Columbia Offset, Singapore
Printed by Mandarin Offset (HK) Limited, Hong Kong
Distributed by Sidgwick & Jackson Limited, London

LEAR
King of Britain

EARL OF KENT
disguised as Lear's servant

FOOL
Lear's jester

IAN POLLOCK

CORDELIA
Lear's youngest daughter

KING OF FRANCE
Cordelia's husband

DUKE OF BURGUNDY
Cordelia's Suitor

REGAN
Lear's second daughter

GONERIL
Lear's eldest daughter

Duke of CORNWALL
Regan's husband

DUKE OF ALBANY
Goneril's husband

OSWALD
Goneril's steward

CURAN
a courtier

GENTLE MAN

EARL OF GLOUCESTER

EDGAR
Gloucester's legitimate son

EDMUND
Gloucester's bastard son

THE TRAGEDY OF KING LEAR

King Lear's tragedy is a fall from the heights of power to the depths of powerlessness. But it is also an ascent from ignorance into knowledge. The unmaking of Lear the king, is the making of Lear the man.

The possession of absolute power has shielded Lear from reality. It has kept him in a world of fantasy: a royal command performance in which everyone is forced to act a part, because the king has not grown out of playing god. He does not know what it is like to live without power. Because he is ignorant of real life, he imagines that what is natural is what is obedient to his will: he has put himself <u>above nature.</u> To give up his powerful position means for the first time being obliged to step down into the real and natural world. His abdication is a step over a precipice.

The tragedy is not confined to this one man, for, as king, he is the source of earthly authority, the kingpin of the whole state. It is the king who has distorted nature from its course, holding it fast by the locks and dams of his power and ignorance. Once they are blown, the whole state is in danger of being swept away, and the bonds broken between allies, brothers, sisters, host and guest, master and servant, wife and husband, parent and child. If what is wrong is to be put right, the upheaval must be immense. Even the meaning of words, sanity in the mind, and harmony among the elements must be dissolved before the world can be put back together again. Everything is swept up in a storm like the unprecedented windstorm of 1606 (the year of King Lear's writing), which left a trail of destruction over England and northern Europe. In such a storm of nature wreaking its revenge, Lear becomes a victim of the very sufferings which once his power inflicted. He had reduced others to mere objects, so now is he; now is <u>he</u> dispossessed, banished, reduced to beggary. And his taskmaster is a Fool – the court jester who is permitted to tell truths to the mighty, but only if truth can be served up as entertainment.

As Lear falls into the terrible truth beneath appearances, he becomes, himself, the Fool. And so devastating is his experience of the cruel world that he longs to see it destroyed. When he was surrounded by lies, he believed everything: now, surrounded by the truth, he can believe in nothing. That 'Nothing' which has haunted him since the moment of his fall at last possesses him.

Only as he dies does he rise again to the heights of belief – in a moment of towering illusion. For he has learned compassion. He has learned to give the thing he once could only take: love. In death, his last feeling is one of joy that <u>someone else</u> should be restored to life. Out of the selfish comes the selfless; out of great suffering comes great hope. By the life and death of this old man, we that are young are challenged to know ourselves and our world.

David Gibson

THE STORY

In old age, **King Lear** has decided to retire and divide his kingdom between his three daughters, giving the best portion to the one who loves him most.

Goneril and **Regan** declare great love, but **Cordelia,** his favourite, simply says that she loves him as a daughter should. Enraged, Lear banishes her, and also **Kent,** who intervenes on her behalf. Cordelia leaves Britain to marry the **King of France,** and Lear splits her inheritance between the others, on condition they maintain him and his knights.

Edmund, bastard son of the old Earl of **Gloucester,** schemes to gain his father's land and title from **Edgar,** the legitimate son and heir. He forges a letter in Edgar's name; Gloucester believes the lies it contains, and Edgar is forced to flee.

Lear's daughters tire of his autocratic behaviour, and deny him all privileges. In fury and despair Lear rushes into the night with his **Fool,** where they are caught in a terrible storm. Found by Kent they take refuge in a hovel, and inside encounter Edgar disguised as "Tom", a lunatic beggar. Lear, his mind now unhinged, conducts a mock trial of his ungrateful daughters.

Gloucester learns that Lear's life is threatened by his daughters, and he provides him with food and means of escape. Regan and her husband, **Cornwall,** discover Gloucester's complicity, and gouge out his eyes. Cornwall is stabbed by a servant.

News of Lear's plight brings Cordelia back from France with an army. Edmund and **Albany,** Goneril's husband, lead a force to fight the French at Dover. Goneril, who is in love with Edmund, plans to get rid of her husband. But Regan, now a widow, wants Edmund too and the sisters turn against each other.

The blind Gloucester is led to Dover by his son Edgar, still in disguise. To protect his father Edgar kills **Oswald,** Goneril's treacherous steward, and on the body finds her letter urging Edmund to kill her husband.

Cordelia is re-united with her father, but her troops lose the battle. She and Lear are imprisoned by Edmund, who orders their death. Goneril poisons Regan. Edmund is challenged to a duel by an unknown knight, and fatally wounded. Seeing Edmund dying, and confronted with her incriminating letter, Goneril commits suicide. The unknown knight is revealed as Edgar. But for Cordelia and her father release comes too late. Cordelia has been hanged, and Lear dies of grief.

ACT 1, SCENE 1 : KING LEAR'S PALACE

ENTER GLOUCESTER AND KENT

I THOUGHT THE KING HAD MORE AFFECTED THE DUKE OF ALBANY THAN CORNWALL.

IT DID ALWAYS SEEM SO TO US. BUT NOW, IN THE DIVISION OF THE KINGDOM, IT APPEARS NOT WHICH OF THE DUKES HE VALUES MOST, FOR EQUALITIES ARE SO WEIGHED THAT CURIOSITY IN NEITHER CAN MAKE CHOICE OF EITHER'S MOIETY.

ENTER EDMUND

IS NOT THIS YOUR SON, MY LORD?

HIS BREEDING, SIR, HATH BEEN AT MY CHARGE. I HAVE SO OFTEN BLUSHED TO ACKNOWLEDGE HIM THAT NOW I AM BRAZED TO 'T.

I CANNOT CONCEIVE YOU.

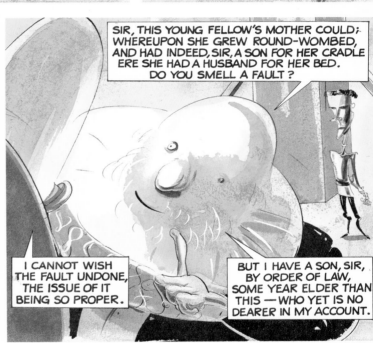

SIR, THIS YOUNG FELLOW'S MOTHER COULD; WHEREUPON SHE GREW ROUND-WOMBED, AND HAD INDEED, SIR, A SON FOR HER CRADLE ERE SHE HAD A HUSBAND FOR HER BED. DO YOU SMELL A FAULT?

I CANNOT WISH THE FAULT UNDONE, THE ISSUE OF IT BEING SO PROPER.

BUT I HAVE A SON, SIR, BY ORDER OF LAW, SOME YEAR ELDER THAN THIS — WHO YET IS NO DEARER IN MY ACCOUNT.

THOUGH THIS KNAVE CAME SOMETHING SAUCILY TO THE WORLD, BEFORE HE WAS SENT FOR, YET WAS HIS MOTHER FAIR, THERE WAS GOOD SPORT AT HIS MAKING, AND THE WHORESON MUST BE ACKNOWLEDGED.

DO YOU KNOW THIS NOBLE GENTLEMAN, EDMUND?

NO, MY LORD.

MY LORD OF KENT. REMEMBER HIM HEREAFTER AS MY HONOURABLE FRIEND.

1

MY SERVICES TO YOUR LORDSHIP.

I MUST LOVE YOU AND SUE TO KNOW YOU BETTER.

SIR, I SHALL STUDY DESERVING.

HE HATH BEEN OUT NINE YEARS — AND AWAY HE SHALL AGAIN.

THE KING IS COMING!

ENTER KING LEAR, CORDELIA, REGAN, CORNWALL, GONERIL, ALBANY

ATTEND THE LORDS OF FRANCE AND BURGUNDY, GLOUCESTER.

I SHALL, MY LORD.

MEANTIME WE SHALL EXPRESS OUR DARKER PURPOSE.

GIVE ME THE MAP THERE.

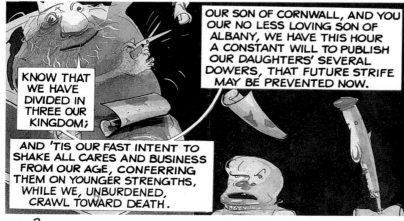

KNOW THAT WE HAVE DIVIDED IN THREE OUR KINGDOM;

AND 'TIS OUR FAST INTENT TO SHAKE ALL CARES AND BUSINESS FROM OUR AGE, CONFERRING THEM ON YOUNGER STRENGTHS, WHILE WE, UNBURDENED, CRAWL TOWARD DEATH.

OUR SON OF CORNWALL, AND YOU OUR NO LESS LOVING SON OF ALBANY, WE HAVE THIS HOUR A CONSTANT WILL TO PUBLISH OUR DAUGHTERS' SEVERAL DOWERS, THAT FUTURE STRIFE MAY BE PREVENTED NOW.

THE PRINCES, FRANCE AND BURGUNDY, GREAT RIVALS IN OUR YOUNGEST DAUGHTER'S LOVE, LONG IN OUR COURT HAVE MADE THEIR AMOROUS SOJOURN, AND HERE ARE TO BE ANSWERED.

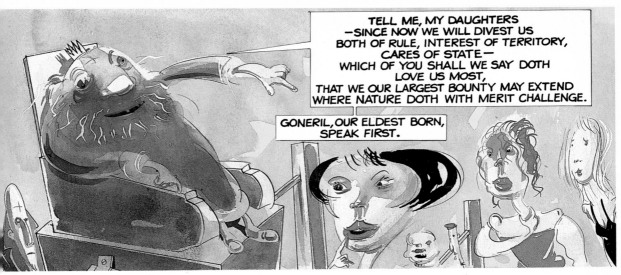

TELL ME, MY DAUGHTERS —SINCE NOW WE WILL DIVEST US BOTH OF RULE, INTEREST OF TERRITORY, CARES OF STATE— WHICH OF YOU SHALL WE SAY DOTH LOVE US MOST, THAT WE OUR LARGEST BOUNTY MAY EXTEND WHERE NATURE DOTH WITH MERIT CHALLENGE.

GONERIL, OUR ELDEST BORN, SPEAK FIRST.

SIR, I LOVE YOU MORE THAN WORD CAN WIELD THE MATTER; DEARER THAN EYESIGHT, SPACE AND LIBERTY; BEYOND WHAT CAN BE VALUED RICH OR RARE; NO LESS THAN LIFE, WITH GRACE, HEALTH, BEAUTY, HONOUR; AS MUCH AS CHILD E'ER LOVED OR FATHER FOUND;

A LOVE THAT MAKES BREATH POOR AND SPEECH UNABLE; BEYOND ALL MANNER OF "SO MUCH" I LOVE YOU.

WHAT SHALL CORDELIA SPEAK?

LOVE, AND BE SILENT.

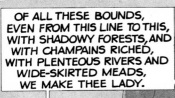

OF ALL THESE BOUNDS, EVEN FROM THIS LINE TO THIS, WITH SHADOWY FORESTS, AND WITH CHAMPAINS RICHED, WITH PLENTEOUS RIVERS AND WIDE-SKIRTED MEADS, WE MAKE THEE LADY.

TO THINE AND ALBANY'S ISSUES, BE THIS PERPETUAL.

WHAT SAYS OUR SECOND DAUGHTER, OUR DEAREST REGAN, WIFE OF CORNWALL?

I AM MADE OF THAT SELF METAL AS MY SISTER, AND PRIZE ME AT HER WORTH; IN MY TRUE HEART I FIND SHE NAMES MY VERY DEED OF LOVE;

ONLY SHE COMES TOO SHORT, THAT I PROFESS MYSELF AN ENEMY TO ALL OTHER JOYS WHICH THE MOST PRECIOUS SQUARE OF SENSE POSSESSES, AND FIND I AM ALONE FELICITATE IN YOU DEAR HIGHNESS' LOVE.

THEN POOR CORDELIA!

AND YET NOT SO, SINCE I AM SURE MY LOVE'S MORE PONDEROUS THAN MY TONGUE.

3

TO THEE AND THINE, HEREDITARY EVER, REMAIN THIS AMPLE THIRD OF OUR FAIR KINGDOM

-NO LESS IN SPACE, VALIDITY AND PLEASURE THAN THAT CONFERRED ON GONERIL.

NOW, OUR JOY, ALTHOUGH OUR LAST AND LEAST, TO WHOSE YOUNG LOVE THE VINES OF FRANCE AND MILK OF BURGUNDY STRIVE TO BE INTERESTED –

WHAT CAN YOU SAY TO DRAW A THIRD MORE OPULENT THAN YOUR SISTERS'?

SPEAK.

NOTHING MY LORD.

NOTHING ?

NOTHING.

NOTHING WILL COME OF NOTHING.

SPEAK AGAIN.

UNHAPPY THAT I AM, I CANNOT HEAVE MY HEART INTO MY MOUTH.

I LOVE YOUR MAJESTY ACCORDING TO MY BOND.

NO MORE NOR LESS.

HOW NOW, CORDELIA ? MEND YOUR SPEECH A LITTLE, LEST YOU MAY MAR YOUR FORTUNES.

GOOD MY LORD, YOU HAVE BEGOT ME, BRED ME, LOVED ME. I RETURN THOSE DUTIES BACK AS ARE RIGHT FIT, OBEY YOU, LOVE YOU, AND MOST HONOUR YOU;

WHY HAVE MY SISTERS HUSBANDS, IF THEY SAY THEY LOVE YOU ALL ? HAPLY, WHEN I SHALL WED, THAT LORD WHOSE HAND MUST TAKE MY PLIGHT SHALL CARRY HALF MY LOVE WITH HIM, HALF MY CARE AND DUTY.

SURE I SHALL NEVER MARRY LIKE MY SISTERS, TO LOVE MY FATHER ALL.

BUT GOES THY HEART WITH THIS ?

AY, MY GOOD LORD.

SO YOUNG, AND SO UNTENDER ?

SO YOUNG, MY LORD, AND TRUE.

LET IT BE SO!

THY TRUTH, THEN, BE THY DOWER!

FOR BY THE SACRED RADIANCE OF THE SUN, THE MYSTERIES OF HECAT AND THE NIGHT,

BY ALL THE OPERATION OF THE ORBS FROM WHOM WE DO EXIST AND CEASE TO BE,

HERE I DISCLAIM ALL MY PATERNAL CARE, PROPINQUITY AND PROPERTY OF BLOOD, AND AS A STRANGER TO MY HEART AND ME HOLD THEE, FROM THIS, FOR EVER.

THE BARBAROUS SCYTHIAN, OR HE THAT MAKES HIS GENERATION MESSES TO GORGE HIS APPETITE, SHALL TO MY BOSOM BE AS WELL NEIGHBOURED, PITIED, AND RELIEVED AS THOU MY SOMETIME DAUGHTER.

GOOD MY LIEGE —

PEACE, KENT!

COME NOT BETWEEN THE DRAGON AND HIS WRATH. I LOVED HER MOST, AND THOUGHT TO SET MY REST ON HER KIND NURSERY.

HENCE AND AVOID MY SIGHT !

SO BE MY GRAVE MY PEACE AS HERE I GIVE HER FATHER'S HEART FROM HER.

CALL FRANCE !

WHO STIRS ?

CALL BURGUNDY !

CORNWALL AND ALBANY, WITH MY TWO DAUGHTERS' DOWERS DIGEST THE THIRD. LET PRIDE, WHICH SHE CALLS PLAINNESS, MARRY HER.

I DO INVEST YOU JOINTLY WITH MY POWER, PRE-EMINENCE AND ALL THE LARGE EFFECTS THAT TROOP WITH MAJESTY.

OURSELF, BY MONTHLY COURSE, WITH RESERVATION OF AN HUNDRED KNIGHTS BY YOU TO BE SUSTAINED, SHALL OUR ABODE MAKE WITH YOU BY DUE TURN.

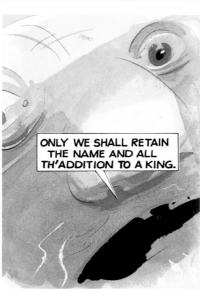

ONLY WE SHALL RETAIN THE NAME AND ALL TH'ADDITION TO A KING.

THE SWAY, REVENUE, EXECUTION OF THE REST, BELOVED SONS, BE YOURS. WHICH TO CONFIRM, THIS CORONET PART BETWEEN YOU.

ROYAL LEAR, WHOM I HAVE EVER HONOURED AS MY KING, LOVED AS MY FATHER, AS MY MASTER FOLLOWED, AS MY GREAT PATRON THOUGHT ON IN MY PRAYERS –

THE BOW IS BENT AND DRAWN; MAKE FROM THE SHAFT !

LET IT FALL RATHER, THOUGH THE FORK INVADE THE REGION OF MY HEART.

BE KENT UNMANNERLY WHEN LEAR IS MAD. WHAT WOULD'ST THOU DO, OLD MAN ?

THINK'ST THOU THAT DUTY SHALL HAVE DREAD TO SPEAK, WHEN POWER TO FLATTERY BOWS ?

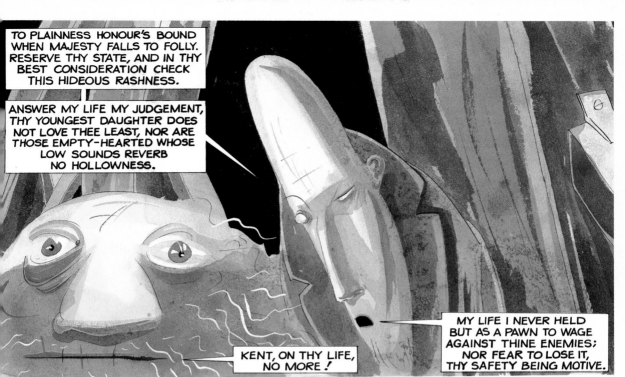

TO PLAINNESS HONOUR'S BOUND WHEN MAJESTY FALLS TO FOLLY. RESERVE THY STATE, AND IN THY BEST CONSIDERATION CHECK THIS HIDEOUS RASHNESS.

ANSWER MY LIFE MY JUDGEMENT, THY YOUNGEST DAUGHTER DOES NOT LOVE THEE LEAST, NOR ARE THOSE EMPTY-HEARTED WHOSE LOW SOUNDS REVERB NO HOLLOWNESS.

KENT, ON THY LIFE, NO MORE!

MY LIFE I NEVER HELD BUT AS A PAWN TO WAGE AGAINST THINE ENEMIES; NOR FEAR TO LOSE IT, THY SAFETY BEING MOTIVE.

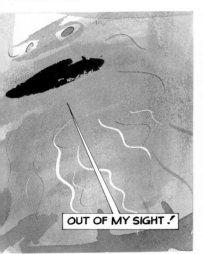

OUT OF MY SIGHT!

SEE BETTER, LEAR, AND LET ME STILL REMAIN THE TRUE BLANK OF THINE EYE.

NOW BY APOLLO—

NOW BY APOLLO, KING, THOU SWEAR'ST THY GODS IN VAIN.

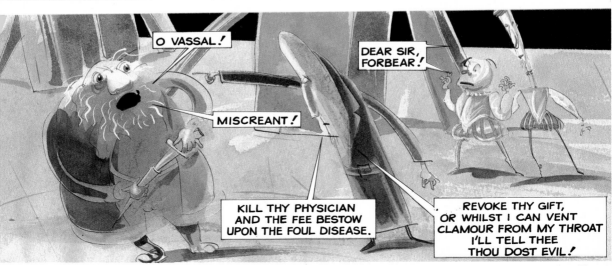

O VASSAL!

MISCREANT!

DEAR SIR, FORBEAR!

KILL THY PHYSICIAN AND THE FEE BESTOW UPON THE FOUL DISEASE.

REVOKE THY GIFT, OR WHILST I CAN VENT CLAMOUR FROM MY THROAT I'LL TELL THEE THOU DOST EVIL!

HEAR ME, RECREANT! ON THINE ALLEGIANCE, HEAR ME!

THAT THOU HAST SOUGHT TO MAKE US BREAK OUR VOWS—WHICH WE DURST NEVER YET—AND, WITH STRAINED PRIDE, TO COME BETWIXT OUR SENTENCE AND OUR POWER—WHICH NOR OUR NATURE NOR OUR PLACE CAN BEAR—OUR POTENCY MADE GOOD, TAKE THY REWARD.

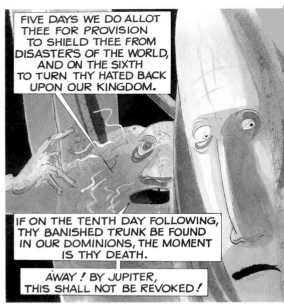

FIVE DAYS WE DO ALLOT THEE FOR PROVISION TO SHIELD THEE FROM DISASTERS OF THE WORLD, AND ON THE SIXTH TO TURN THY HATED BACK UPON OUR KINGDOM.

IF ON THE TENTH DAY FOLLOWING, THY BANISHED TRUNK BE FOUND IN OUR DOMINIONS, THE MOMENT IS THY DEATH.

AWAY! BY JUPITER, THIS SHALL NOT BE REVOKED!

FARE THEE WELL, KING; SITH THUS THOU WILT APPEAR,

FREEDOM LIVES HENCE AND BANISHMENT IS HERE.

THE GODS TO THEIR DEAR SHELTER TAKE THEE, MAID, THAT JUSTLY THINK'ST AND HAST MOST RIGHTLY SAID.

AND YOUR LARGE SPEECHES MAY YOUR DEEDS APPROVE, THAT GOOD EFFECTS MAY SPRING FROM WORDS OF LOVE.

THUS KENT, O PRINCES BIDS YOU ALL ADIEU!

HE'LL SHAPE HIS OLD COURSE IN A COUNTRY NEW.

HERE'S FRANCE AND BURGUNDY, MY NOBLE LORD.

MY LORD OF BURGUNDY, WE FIRST ADDRESS TOWARD YOU, WHO WITH THIS KING HATH RIVALLED FOR OUR DAUGHTER: WHAT IN THE LEAST WILL YOU REQUIRE IN PRESENT DOWER WITH HER, OR CEASE YOUR QUEST OF LOVE?

MOST ROYAL MAJESTY, I CRAVE NO MORE THAN HATH YOUR HIGHNESS OFFERED, NOR WILL YOU TENDER LESS.

RIGHT NOBLE BURGUNDY, WHEN SHE WAS DEAR TO US, WE DID HOLD HER SO; BUT NOW HER PRICE IS FALLEN. SIR, THERE SHE STANDS.

IF AUGHT WITHIN THAT LITTLE-SEEMING SUBSTANCE, OR ALL OF IT, WITH OUR DISPLEASURE PIECED, AND NOTHING MORE, MAY FITLY LIKE YOUR GRACE, SHE'S THERE AND SHE IS YOURS.

I KNOW NO ANSWER.

WILL YOU, WITH THOSE INFIRMITIES SHE OWES, UNFRIENDED, NEW-ADOPTED TO OUR HATE, DOWERED WITH OUR CURSE AND STRANGERED WITH OUR OATH, TAKE HER OR LEAVE HER?

PARDON ME, ROYAL SIR, ELECTION MAKES NOT UP IN SUCH CONDITIONS.

THEN LEAVE HER, SIR; FOR BY THE POWER THAT MADE ME, I TELL YOU ALL HER WEALTH.

FOR YOU, GREAT KING, I WOULD NOT FROM YOUR LOVE MAKE SUCH A STRAY TO MATCH YOU WHERE I HATE; THEREFORE BESEECH YOU T'AVERT YOUR LIKING A MORE WORTHIER WAY THAN ON A WRETCH WHOM NATURE IS ASHAMED ALMOST T'ACKNOWLEDGE HERS.

THIS IS MOST STRANGE THAT SHE WHOM EVEN BUT NOW WAS YOUR BEST OBJECT, THE ARGUMENT OF YOUR PRAISE, BALM OF YOUR AGE, THE BEST, THE DEAREST, SHOULD IN THIS TRICE OF TIME COMMIT A THING SO MONSTROUS TO DISMANTLE SO MANY FOLDS OF FAVOUR.

SURE HER OFFENCE MUST BE OF SUCH UNNATURAL DEGREE THAT MONSTERS IT — OR YOUR FORE-VOUCHED AFFECTION FALL INTO TAINT — WHICH TO BELIEVE OF HER MUST BE A FAITH THAT REASON, WITHOUT MIRACLE, SHOULD NEVER PLANT IN ME.

I YET BESEECH YOUR MAJESTY—

IF FOR I WANT THAT GLIB AND OILY ART TO SPEAK AND PURPOSE NOT (SINCE WHAT I WELL INTEND I'LL DO'T BEFORE I SPEAK)

THAT YOU MAKE KNOWN IT IS NO VICIOUS BLOT, MURDER OR FOULNESS, NO UNCHASTE ACTION OR DISHONOURED STEP THAT HATH DEPRIVED ME OF YOUR GRACE AND FAVOUR,

BUT EVEN FOR WANT OF THAT FOR WHICH I AM RICHER: A STILL-SOLICITING EYE, AND SUCH A TONGUE THAT I AM GLAD I HAVE NOT, THOUGH NOT TO HAVE IT HATH LOST ME IN YOUR LIKING.

BETTER THOU HADST NOT BEEN BORN THAN NOT T'HAVE PLEASED ME BETTER!

IS IT BUT THIS?

—A TARDINESS IN NATURE WHICH OFTEN LEAVES THE HISTORY UNSPOKE THAT IT INTENDS TO DO?

MY LORD OF BURGUNDY, WHAT SAY YOU TO THE LADY? LOVE'S NOT LOVE WHEN IT IS MINGLED WITH REGARDS THAT STANDS ALOOF FROM TH'ENTIRE POINT.

WILL YOU HAVE HER?

SHE IS HERSELF A DOWRY.

ROYAL LEAR, GIVE BUT THAT PORTION WHICH YOURSELF PROPOSED, AND HERE I TAKE CORDELIA BY THE HAND, DUCHESS OF BURGUNDY.

NOTHING! I HAVE SWORN; I AM FIRM.

I AM SORRY THEN YOU HAVE SO LOST A FATHER THAT YOU MUST LOSE A HUSBAND.

PEACE BE WITH BURGUNDY.

SINCE THAT RESPECT AND FORTUNES ARE HIS LOVE, I SHALL NOT BE HIS WIFE.

FAIREST CORDELIA, THAT ART MOST RICH BEING POOR; MOST CHOICE, FORSAKEN; AND MOST LOVED, DESPISED; THEE AND THY VIRTUES HERE I SEIZE UPON. BE IT LAWFUL I TAKE UP WHAT'S CAST AWAY.

GODS, GODS! 'TIS STRANGE THAT FROM THEIR COLD'ST NEGLECT MY LOVE SHOULD KINDLE TO INFLAMED RESPECT.

THY DOWERLESS DAUGHTER, KING, THROWN TO MY CHANCE, IS QUEEN OF US, OF OURS, AND OUR FAIR FRANCE. NOT ALL THE DUKES OF WAT'RISH BURGUNDY CAN BUY THIS UNPRIZED PRECIOUS MAID OF ME.

BID THEM FAREWELL, CORDELIA, THOUGH UNKIND. THOU LOSEST HERE, A BETTER WHERE TO FIND.

THOU HAST HER, FRANCE; LET HER BE THINE, FOR WE HAVE NO SUCH DAUGHTER, NOR SHALL EVER SEE THAT FACE OF HERS AGAIN.

THEREFORE BE GONE, WITHOUT OUR GRACE, OUR LOVE, OUR BENISON!

COME, NOBLE BURGUNDY.

BID FAREWELL TO YOUR SISTERS.

THE JEWELS OF OUR FATHER, WITH WASHED EYES CORDELIA LEAVES YOU.

I KNOW YOU, WHAT YOU ARE; AND LIKE A SISTER, AM MOST LOATH TO CALL YOUR FAULTS AS THEY ARE NAMED.

LOVE WELL OUR FATHER. TO YOUR PROFESSÈD BOSOMS I COMMIT HIM.

BUT YET, ALAS, STOOD I WITHIN HIS GRACE, I WOULD PREFER HIM TO A BETTER PLACE.

SO FAREWELL TO YOU BOTH.

PRESCRIBE NOT US OUR DUTY.

LET YOUR STUDY BE TO CONTENT YOUR LORD, WHO HATH RECEIVED YOU AT FORTUNE'S ALMS.

YOU HAVE OBEDIENCE SCANTED, AND WELL ARE WORTH THE WANT THAT YOU HAVE WANTED.

TIME SHALL UNFOLD WHAT PLIGHTED CUNNING HIDES; WHO COVERS FAULTS, AT LAST WITH SHAME DERIDES.

WELL MAY YOU PROSPER.

COME, MY FAIR CORDELIA.

SISTER, IT IS NOT LITTLE I HAVE TO SAY OF WHAT MOST NEARLY APPERTAINS TO US BOTH. I THINK OUR FATHER WILL HENCE TONIGHT.

THAT'S MOST CERTAIN, AND WITH YOU; NEXT MONTH WITH US.

YOU SEE HOW FULL OF CHANGES HIS AGE IS. THE OBSERVATION WE HAVE MADE OF IT HATH NOT BEEN LITTLE.

HE ALWAYS LOVED OUR SISTER MOST, AND WITH WHAT POOR JUDGEMENT HE HATH NOW CAST HER OFF APPEARS TOO GROSSLY.

'TIS THE INFIRMITY OF HIS AGE. YET HE HATH EVER BUT SLENDERLY KNOWN HIMSELF.

THE BEST AND SOUNDEST OF HIS TIME HATH BEEN BUT RASH. THEN MUST WE LOOK FROM HIS AGE TO RECEIVE NOT ALONE THE IMPERFECTIONS OF LONG-INGRAFFED CONDITION, BUT THEREWITHAL THE UNRULY WAYWARDNESS THAT INFIRM AND CHOLERIC YEARS BRING WITH THEM.

SUCH UNCONSTANT STARTS ARE WE LIKE TO HAVE FROM HIM AS THIS OF KENT'S BANISHMENT.

THERE IS FURTHER COMPLIMENT OF LEAVE-TAKING BETWEEN FRANCE AND HIM.

PRAY YOU, LET US HIT TOGETHER. IF OUR FATHER CARRY AUTHORITY WITH SUCH DISPOSITION AS HE BEARS, THIS LAST SURRENDER OF HIS WILL BUT OFFEND US.

WE SHALL FURTHER THINK OF IT.

WE MUST DO SOMETHING, AND I' TH' HEAT!

13

ENTER GLOUCESTER

KENT BANISHED THUS?
AND FRANCE IN CHOLER PARTED?
AND THE KING GONE TONIGHT?
PRESCRIBED HIS POWER?
CONFINED TO EXHIBITION?
ALL THIS DONE UPON THE GAD!

EDMUND, HOW NOW! WHAT NEWS?

SO PLEASE YOUR LORDSHIP, NONE.

WHY SO EARNESTLY SEEK YOU TO PUT UP THAT LETTER?

I KNOW NO NEWS, MY LORD.

WHAT PAPER WERE YOU READING?

NOTHING, MY LORD.

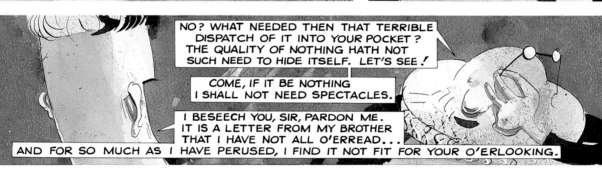

NO? WHAT NEEDED THEN THAT TERRIBLE DISPATCH OF IT INTO YOUR POCKET? THE QUALITY OF NOTHING HATH NOT SUCH NEED TO HIDE ITSELF. LET'S SEE!

COME, IF IT BE NOTHING I SHALL NOT NEED SPECTACLES.

I BESEECH YOU, SIR, PARDON ME. IT IS A LETTER FROM MY BROTHER THAT I HAVE NOT ALL O'ERREAD...

AND FOR SO MUCH AS I HAVE PERUSED, I FIND IT NOT FIT FOR YOUR O'ERLOOKING.

GIVE ME THE LETTER, SIR!

I SHALL OFFEND EITHER TO DETAIN OR GIVE IT...

THE CONTENTS, AS IN PART I UNDERSTAND THEM, ARE TO BLAME.

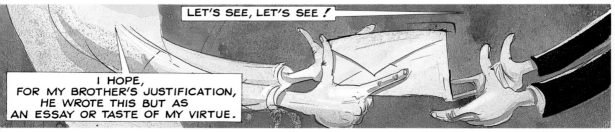

LET'S SEE, LET'S SEE!

I HOPE, FOR MY BROTHER'S JUSTIFICATION, HE WROTE THIS BUT AS AN ESSAY OR TASTE OF MY VIRTUE.

15

This policy and reverence of age makes the world bitter to the best of our times; keeps our fortunes from us till our oldness cannot relish them.

I begin to find an idle and fond bondage in the oppression of aged tyranny, who sways, not as it hath power, but as it is suffered.

Come to me, that of this I may speak more. If our father would sleep till I waked him, you should enjoy half his revenue for ever, and live the beloved of your brother

Edgar ~

HUM! CONSPIRACY! "SLEEP TILL I WAKED HIM"? "YOU SHOULD ENJOY HALF HIS REVENUE"? MY SON EDGAR?

HAD HE A HAND TO WRITE THIS? A HEART AND BRAIN TO BREED IT IN?

WHEN CAME YOU TO THIS? WHO BROUGHT IT?

IT WAS NOT BROUGHT ME, MY LORD; THERE'S THE CUNNING OF IT; I FOUND IT THROWN IN AT THE CASEMENT OF MY CLOSET.

YOU KNOW THE CHARACTER TO BE YOUR BROTHER'S?

IF THE MATTER WERE GOOD, MY LORD, I DURST SWEAR IT WERE HIS; BUT, IN RESPECT OF THAT, I WOULD FAIN THINK IT WERE NOT.

IT *IS* HIS!

IT IS HIS HAND, MY LORD; BUT I HOPE HIS HEART IS NOT IN THE CONTENTS.

HAS HE NEVER BEFORE SOUNDED YOU IN THIS BUSINESS?

NEVER, MY LORD.

BUT I HAVE HEARD HIM OFT MAINTAIN IT TO BE FIT THAT, SONS AT PERFECT AGE, AND FATHERS DECLINED, THE FATHER SHOULD BE AS WARD TO THE SON, AND THE SON MANAGE HIS REVENUE.

O VILLAIN, VILLAIN! HIS VERY OPINION IN THE LETTER!

ABHORRÈD VILLAIN! UNNATURAL, DETESTED, BRUTISH VILLAIN! WORSE THAN BRUTISH!

GO, SIRRAH, SEEK HIM; I'LL APPREHEND HIM. ABOMINABLE VILLAIN! WHERE IS HE?

I DO NOT WELL KNOW, MY LORD.

IF IT SHALL PLEASE YOU TO SUSPEND YOUR INDIGNATION AGAINST MY BROTHER TILL YOU CAN DERIVE FROM HIM BETTER TESTIMONY OF HIS INTENT, YOU SHALL RUN A CERTAIN COURSE;

WHERE, IF YOU VIOLENTLY PROCEED AGAINST HIM, MISTAKING HIS PURPOSE, IT WOULD MAKE A GREAT GAP IN YOUR OWN HONOUR AND SHAKE IN PIECES THE HEART OF HIS OBEDIENCE.

I DARE PAWN DOWN MY LIFE FOR HIM, THAT HE HATH WRIT THIS TO FEEL MY AFFECTION TO YOUR HONOUR, AND TO NO OTHER PRETENCE OF DANGER.

THINK YOU SO?

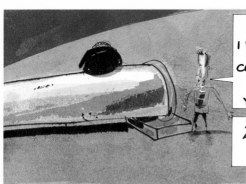

IF YOUR HONOUR JUDGE IT MEET, I WILL PLACE YOU WHERE YOU SHALL HEAR US CONFER OF THIS, AND BY AN AURICULAR ASSURANCE HAVE YOUR SATISFACTION;

AND THAT WITHOUT ANY FURTHER DELAY THAN THIS VERY EVENING.

HE CANNOT BE SUCH A MONSTER—

NOR IS NOT, SURE.

— TO HIS FATHER, THAT SO TENDERLY AND ENTIRELY LOVES HIM.

HEAVEN AND EARTH!

EDMUND, SEEK HIM OUT; WIND ME INTO HIM, I PRAY YOU. FRAME THE BUSINESS AFTER YOUR OWN WISDOM.

I WOULD UNSTATE MYSELF TO BE IN A DUE RESOLUTION.

I WILL SEEK HIM, SIR, PRESENTLY, CONVEY THE BUSINESS AS I SHALL FIND MEANS, AND ACQUAINT YOU WITHAL.

THESE LATE ECLIPSES IN THE SUN AND MOON PORTEND NO GOOD TO US: THOUGH THE WISDOM OF NATURE CAN REASON IT THUS AND THUS, YET NATURE FINDS ITSELF SCOURGED BY THE SEQUENT EFFECTS.

LOVE COOLS, FRIENDSHIP FALLS OFF, BROTHERS DIVIDE; IN CITIES, MUTINIES; IN COUNTRIES, DISCORD; IN PALACES, TREASON; AND THE BOND CRACKED 'TWIXT SON AND FATHER.

THIS VILLAIN OF MINE COMES UNDER THE PREDICTION: THERE'S SON AGAINST FATHER. THE KING FALLS FROM BIAS OF NATURE: THERE'S FATHER AGAINST CHILD.

WE HAVE SEEN THE BEST OF OUR TIME: MACHINATIONS, HOLLOWNESS, TREACHERY, AND ALL RUINOUS DISORDERS FOLLOW US DISQUIETLY TO OUR GRAVES.

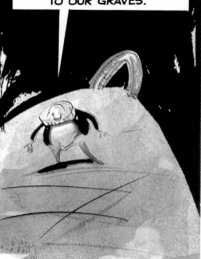

FIND OUT THIS VILLAIN, EDMUND; IT SHALL LOSE THEE NOTHING. DO IT CAREFULLY.

AND THE NOBLE AND TRUE-HEARTED KENT BANISHED! HIS OFFENCE — HONESTY!

'TIS STRANGE.

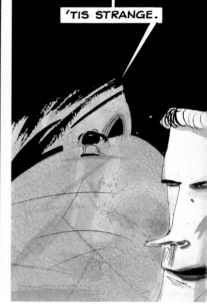

THIS IS THE EXCELLENT FOPPERY OF THE WORLD, THAT, WHEN WE ARE SICK IN FORTUNE (OFTEN THE SURFEITS OF OUR OWN BEHAVIOUR) WE MAKE GUILTY OF OUR DISASTERS THE SUN, THE MOON, AND STARS.

AS IF WE WERE VILLAINS ON NECESSITY, FOOLS BY HEAVENLY COMPULSION, KNAVES, THIEVES AND TREACHERS BY SPHERICAL PREDOMINANCE; DRUNKARDS, LIARS AND ADULTERERS BY AN ENFORCED OBEDIENCE OF PLANETARY INFLUENCE; AND ALL THAT WE ARE EVIL IN, BY A DIVINE THRUSTING-ON.

AN ADMIRABLE EVASION OF WHOREMASTER MAN, TO LAY HIS GOATISH DISPOSITION TO THE CHARGE OF A STAR!

MY FATHER COMPOUNDED WITH MY MOTHER UNDER THE DRAGON'S TAIL, AND MY NATIVITY WAS UNDER *URSA MAJOR*;

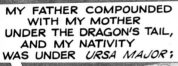

SO THAT IT FOLLOWS I AM ROUGH AND LECHEROUS.

FUT! I SHOULD HAVE BEEN THAT I AM HAD THE MAIDENLIEST STAR IN THE FIRMAMENT TWINKLED ON MY BASTARDIZING.

EDGAR —

ENTER EDGAR

AND PAT HE COMES, LIKE THE CATASTROPHE OF THE OLD COMEDY!

MY CUE IS VILLANOUS MELANCHOLY, WITH A SIGH LIKE TOM O'BEDLAM.

O, THESE ECLIPSES DO PORTEND THESE DIVISIONS!

FA!

SOL!

LA!

MI!

HOW NOW, BROTHER EDMUND! WHAT SERIOUS CONTEMPLATION ARE YOU IN?

I AM THINKING, BROTHER, OF A PREDICTION I READ THIS OTHER DAY, WHAT SHOULD FOLLOW THESE ECLIPSES.

DO YOU BUSY YOURSELF WITH THAT?

I PROMISE YOU, THE EFFECTS HE WRITES OF SUCCEED UNHAPPILY; AS OF UNNATURALNESS BETWEEN THE CHILD AND THE PARENT; DEATH, DEARTH, DISSOLUTIONS OF ANCIENT AMITIES; DIVISIONS IN STATE; MENACES AND MALEDICTIONS AGAINST KING AND NOBLES;

NEEDLESS DIFFIDENCES, BANISHMENT OF FRIENDS, DISSIPATION OF COHORTS, NUPTIAL BREACHES, AND I KNOW NOT WHAT.

HOW LONG HAVE YOU BEEN A SECTARY ASTRONOMICAL?

WHEN SAW YOU MY FATHER LAST?

THE NIGHT GONE BY.

SPAKE YOU WITH HIM?

AY, TWO HOURS TOGETHER.

PARTED YOU IN GOOD TERMS?

FOUND YOU NO DISPLEASURE IN HIM, BY WORD OR COUNTENANCE?

NONE AT ALL.

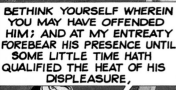

BETHINK YOURSELF WHEREIN YOU MAY HAVE OFFENDED HIM; AND AT MY ENTREATY FOREBEAR HIS PRESENCE UNTIL SOME LITTLE TIME HATH QUALIFIED THE HEAT OF HIS DISPLEASURE,

WHICH AT THIS INSTANT SO RAGETH IN HIM THAT WITH THE MISCHIEF OF YOUR PERSON IT WOULD SCARCELY ALLAY.

SOME VILLAIN HATH DONE ME WRONG.

THAT'S MY FEAR. I PRAY YOU HAVE A CONTINENT FORBEARANCE TILL THE SPEED OF HIS RAGE GOES SLOWER, AND, AS I SAY, RETIRE WITH ME TO MY LODGING, FROM WHENCE I WILL FITLY BRING YOU TO HEAR MY LORD SPEAK.

PRAY YE, GO. THERE'S MY KEY.

IF YOU DO STIR ABROAD, GO ARMED.

ARMED, BROTHER?

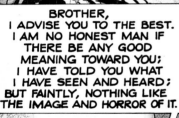

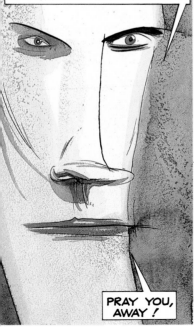

BROTHER, I ADVISE YOU TO THE BEST. I AM NO HONEST MAN IF THERE BE ANY GOOD MEANING TOWARD YOU; I HAVE TOLD YOU WHAT I HAVE SEEN AND HEARD; BUT FAINTLY, NOTHING LIKE THE IMAGE AND HORROR OF IT.

PRAY YOU, AWAY!

SHALL I HEAR FROM YOU ANON?

I DO SERVE YOU IN THIS BUSINESS.

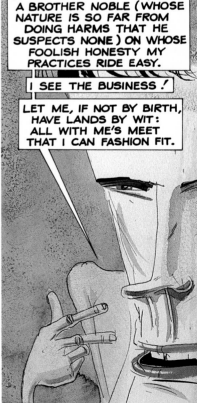

A CREDULOUS FATHER, AND A BROTHER NOBLE (WHOSE NATURE IS SO FAR FROM DOING HARMS THAT HE SUSPECTS NONE) ON WHOSE FOOLISH HONESTY MY PRACTICES RIDE EASY.

I SEE THE BUSINESS!

LET ME, IF NOT BY BIRTH, HAVE LANDS BY WIT: ALL WITH ME'S MEET THAT I CAN FASHION FIT.

DID MY FATHER STRIKE MY GENTLEMAN FOR CHIDING OF HIS FOOL?

AY, MADAM.

BY DAY AND NIGHT, HE WRONGS ME; EVERY HOUR HE FLASHES INTO ONE GROSS CRIME OR OTHER THAT SETS US ALL AT ODDS! I'LL NOT ENDURE IT!

HIS KNIGHTS GROW RIOTOUS, AND HIMSELF UPBRAIDS US ON EVERY TRIFLE.

WHEN HE RETURNS FROM HUNTING, I WILL NOT SPEAK WITH HIM. SAY I AM SICK. IF YOU COME SLACK OF FORMER SERVICES, YOU SHALL DO WELL. THE FAULT OF IT I'LL ANSWER.

HE'S COMING, MADAM.

I HEAR HIM.

PUT ON WHAT WEARY NEGLIGENCE YOU PLEASE, YOU AND YOUR FELLOWS; I'D HAVE IT COME TO QUESTION. IF HE DISTASTE IT, LET HIM TO MY SISTER, WHOSE MIND AND MINE I KNOW, IN THAT, ARE ONE:

NOT TO BE OVER-RULED.

IDLE OLD MAN, THAT STILL WOULD MANAGE THOSE AUTHORITIES THAT HE HATH GIVEN AWAY! NOW, BY MY LIFE, OLD FOOLS ARE BABES AGAIN, AND MUST BE USED WITH CHECKS AS FLATTERIES, WHEN THEY ARE SEEN ABUSED.

REMEMBER WHAT I HAVE SAID.

WELL, MADAM.

AND LET HIS KNIGHTS HAVE COLDER LOOKS AMONG YOU; WHAT GROWS OF IT, NO MATTER. ADVISE YOUR FELLOWS SO.

I WOULD BREED FROM HENCE OCCASIONS, AND I SHALL, THAT I MAY SPEAK. I'LL WRITE STRAIGHT TO MY SISTER TO HOLD MY VERY COURSE. PREPARE FOR DINNER.

IF BUT AS WELL I OTHER ACCENTS BORROW, THAT CAN MY SPEECH DEFUSE, MY GOOD INTENT MAY CARRY THROUGH ITSELF TO THAT FULL ISSUE FOR WHICH I RAZED MY LIKENESS.

NOW, BANISHED KENT, IF THOU CANST SERVE WHERE THOU DOST STAND CONDEMNED, SO MAY IT COME THY MASTER, WHOM THOU LOV'ST, SHALL FIND THEE FULL OF LABOURS.

LET ME NOT STAY A JOT FOR DINNER! GO, GET IT READY!

HOW NOW, WHAT ART THOU?

A MAN, SIR.

WHAT DOST THOU PROFESS? WHAT WOULD'ST THOU WITH US?

I DO PROFESS TO BE NO LESS THAN I SEEM; TO SERVE HIM TRULY THAT WILL PUT ME IN TRUST; TO LOVE HIM THAT IS HONEST; TO CONVERSE WITH HIM THAT IS WISE AND SAYS LITTLE; TO FEAR JUDGEMENT; TO FIGHT WHEN I CANNOT CHOOSE; AND TO EAT NO FISH.

WHAT ART THOU?

A VERY HONEST-HEARTED FELLOW, AND AS POOR AS THE KING.

IF THOU BE'ST AS POOR FOR A SUBJECT AS HE IS FOR A KING, THOU ART POOR ENOUGH.

WHAT WOULD'ST THOU?

SERVICE.

WHO WOULD'ST THOU SERVE?

YOU.

DOST THOU KNOW ME, FELLOW?

NO, SIR.

BUT YOU HAVE THAT IN YOUR COUNTENANCE WHICH I WOULD FAIN CALL MASTER.

WHAT'S THAT?

AUTHORITY.

WHAT SERVICES CANST THOU DO?

I CAN KEEP HONEST COUNSEL, RIDE, RUN, MAR A CURIOUS TALE IN TELLING IT,

AND DELIVER A PLAIN MESSAGE BLUNTLY. THAT WHICH ORDINARY MEN ARE FIT FOR, I AM QUALIFIED IN; AND THE BEST OF ME IS DILIGENCE.

HOW OLD ART THOU?

NOT SO YOUNG, SIR, TO LOVE A WOMAN FOR SINGING, NOR SO OLD TO DOTE ON HER FOR ANYTHING; I HAVE YEARS ON MY BACK FORTY-EIGHT.

FOLLOW ME. THOU SHALT SERVE ME. IF I LIKE THEE NO WORSE AFTER DINNER, I SHALL NOT PART WITH THEE YET.

DINNER, HO!

DINNER!

WHERE'S MY KNAVE?

MY FOOL?

GO YOU AND CALL MY FOOL HITHER!

ENTER OSWALD

YOU, SIRRAH!

WHERE'S MY DAUGHTER?

SO PLEASE YOU—

EXIT OSWALD

24

WHAT SAYS THE FELLOW THERE? CALL THE CLOTPOLL BACK!

WHERE'S MY FOOL, HO? I THINK THE WORLD'S ASLEEP.

HOW NOW! WHERE'S THAT MONGREL?

HE SAYS, MY LORD, YOUR DAUGHTER IS NOT WELL.

WHY CAME NOT THE SLAVE BACK TO ME WHEN I CALLED HIM?

SIR, HE ANSWERED ME IN THE ROUNDEST MANNER, HE WOULD NOT.

HE WOULD NOT!

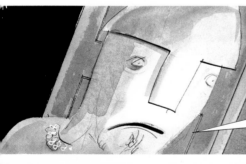

MY LORD, I KNOW NOT WHAT THE MATTER IS; BUT, TO MY JUDGEMENT, YOUR HIGHNESS IS NOT ENTERTAINED WITH THAT CEREMONIOUS AFFECTION AS YOU WERE WONT.

THERE'S A GREAT ABATEMENT OF KINDNESS APPEARS, AS WELL IN THE GENERAL DEPENDANTS AS IN THE DUKE HIMSELF ALSO AND YOUR DAUGHTER.

HA! SAY'ST THOU SO?

I BESEECH YOU, PARDON ME, MY LORD, IF I BE MISTAKEN; FOR MY DUTY CANNOT BE SILENT WHEN I THINK YOUR HIGHNESS WRONGED.

THOU BUT REMEMB'REST ME OF MINE OWN CONCEPTION: I HAVE PERCEIVED A MOST FAINT NEGLECT OF LATE; WHICH I HAVE RATHER BLAMED AS MINE OWN JEALOUS CURIOSITY THAN AS A VERY PRETENCE AND PURPOSE OF UNKINDNESS:

I WILL LOOK FURTHER INTO'T.

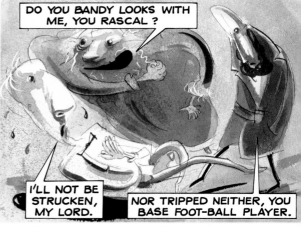

LET ME HIRE HIM TOO.

HERE'S MY COXCOMB.

HOW NOW, MY PRETTY KNAVE! HOW DOST THOU?

SIRRAH, YOU WERE BEST TAKE MY COXCOMB.

WHY, FOOL?

WHY? FOR TAKING ONE'S PART THAT'S OUT OF FAVOUR. NAY, AND THOU CANST NOT SMILE AS THE WIND SITS, THOU'LT CATCH COLD SHORTLY.

THERE, TAKE MY COXCOMB.

WHY, THIS FELLOW HAS BANISHED TWO ON'S DAUGHTERS, AND DID THE THIRD A BLESSING AGAINST HIS WILL: IF THOU FOLLOW HIM THOU MUST NEEDS WEAR MY COXCOMB.

HOW NOW, NUNCLE! WOULD I HAD TWO COXCOMBS, AND TWO DAUGHTERS.

WHY, MY BOY?

IF I GAVE THEM ALL MY LIVING, I'D KEEP MY COXCOMBS MYSELF. THERES MINE; BEG ANOTHER OF THY DAUGHTERS.

TAKE HEED, SIRRAH: THE WHIP!

TRUTH'S A DOG MUST TO KENNEL; HE MUST BE WHIPPED OUT WHEN THE LADY'S BRACH MAY STAND BY TH'FIRE AND STINK.

A PESTILENT GALL TO ME.

SIRRAH, I'LL TEACH THEE A SPEECH.

DO.

MARK IT, NUNCLE.

HAVE MORE THAN THOU SHOWEST, SPEAK LESS THAN THOU KNOWEST, LEND LESS THAN THOU OWEST, RIDE MORE THAN THOU GOEST, LEARN MORE THAN THOU TROWEST, SET LESS THAN THOU THROWEST; LEAVE THY DRINK AND THY WHORE, AND KEEP IN A-DOOR, AND THOU SHALT HAVE MORE THAN TWO TENS TO A SCORE.

27

DOST THOU CALL ME FOOL, BOY?

ALL THY OTHER TITLES THOU HAST GIVEN AWAY; THAT, THOU WAST BORN WITH.

THIS IS NOT ALTOGETHER FOOL, MY LORD.

NO, FAITH, LORDS AND GREAT MEN WILL NOT LET ME.

IF I HAD A MONOPOLY OUT, THEY WOULD HAVE PART ON'T: AND LADIES TOO, THEY WILL NOT LET ME HAVE ALL THE FOOL TO MYSELF; THEY'LL BE SNATCHING.

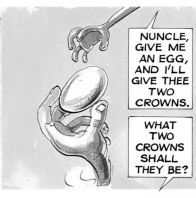

NUNCLE, GIVE ME AN EGG, AND I'LL GIVE THEE TWO CROWNS.

WHAT TWO CROWNS SHALL THEY BE?

WHY, AFTER I HAVE CUT THE EGG I' TH' MIDDLE AND EAT UP THE MEAT—

THE TWO CROWNS OF THE EGG!

WHEN THOU CLOVEST THY CROWN I' TH' MIDDLE, AND GAV'ST AWAY BOTH PARTS, THOU BOR'ST THY ASS ON THY BACK O'ER THE DIRT: THOU HADST LITTLE WIT IN THY BALD CROWN WHEN THOU GAV'ST THY GOLDEN ONE AWAY.

IF I SPEAK LIKE MYSELF IN THIS, LET HIM BE WHIPPED THAT FIRST FINDS IT SO.

FOOLS HAD NE'ER LESS GRACE IN A YEAR, FOR WISE MEN ARE GROWN FOPPISH, AND KNOW NOT HOW THEIR WITS TO WEAR, THEIR MANNERS ARE SO APISH!

WHEN WERE YOU WONT TO BE SO FULL OF SONGS, SIRRAH?

I HAVE USED IT, NUNCLE, E'ER SINCE THOU MAD'ST THY DAUGHTERS THY MOTHERS.

FOR WHEN THOU GAV'ST THEM THE ROD, AND PUT'ST DOWN THINE OWN BREECHES...

THEN THEY FOR SUDDEN JOY DID WEEP, AND I FOR SORROW SUNG, THAT SUCH A KING SHOULD PLAY BO-PEEP, AND GO THE FOOLS AMONG.

PRITHEE, NUNCLE, KEEP A SCHOOLMASTER THAT CAN TEACH THY FOOL TO LIE: I WOULD FAIN LEARN TO LIE.

AND YOU LIE, SIRRAH, WE'LL HAVE YOU WHIPPED!

I MARVEL WHAT KIN THOU AND THY DAUGHTERS ARE.

THEY'LL HAVE ME WHIPPED FOR SPEAKING TRUE, THOU'LT HAVE ME WHIPPED FOR LYING, AND SOMETIMES I AM WHIPPED FOR HOLDING MY PEACE.

I HAD RATHER BE ANY KIND O'THING THAN A FOOL;

AND YET I WOULD NOT BE THEE, NUNCLE; THOU HAST PARED THY WIT O'BOTH SIDES, AND LEFT NOTHING I'TH'MIDDLE!

HERE COMES ONE O'THE PARINGS!

HOW NOW, DAUGHTER! WHAT MAKES THAT FRONTLET ON? YOU ARE TOO MUCH OF LATE I'TH'FROWN.

THOU WAST A PRETTY FELLOW WHEN THOU HADST NO NEED TO CARE FOR HER FROWNING; NOW THOU ART AN O WITHOUT A FIGURE. I AM BETTER THAN THOU ART NOW; I AM A FOOL, THOU ART NOTHING.

YES, FORSOOTH, I WILL HOLD MY TONGUE; SO YOUR FACE BIDS ME, THOUGH YOU SAY NOTHING.

MUM, MUM! HE THAT KEEPS NOR CRUST NOR CRUMB, WEARY OF ALL, SHALL WANT SOME.

THAT'S A SHELLED PEASCOD!

NOT ONLY, SIR, THIS YOUR ALL-LICENSED FOOL, BUT OTHER OF YOUR INSOLENT RETINUE DO HOURLY CARP AND QUARREL, BREAKING FORTH IN RANK AND NOT-TO-BE-ENDURÈD RIOTS.

SIR, I HAD THOUGHT, BY MAKING THIS WELL KNOWN UNTO YOU, TO HAVE FOUND A SAFE REDRESS; BUT NOW GROW FEARFUL, BY WHAT YOURSELF TOO LATE HAVE SPOKE AND DONE, THAT YOU PROTECT THIS COURSE AND PUT IT ON BY YOUR ALLOWANCE.

WHICH IF YOU SHOULD, THE FAULT WOULD NOT 'SCAPE CENSURE, NOR THE REDRESS SLEEP, WHICH, IN THE TENDER OF A WHOLESOME WEAL, MIGHT IN THEIR WORKING DO YOU THAT OFFENCE (WHICH ELSE WERE SHAME) THAT THEN NECESSITY WILL CALL DISCREET PROCEEDING.

FOR YOU KNOW, NUNCLE:

THE HEDGE-SPARROW FED THE CUCKOO SO LONG, THAT IT HAD ITS HEAD BIT OF BY ITS YOUNG.

SO OUT WENT THE CANDLE, AND WE WERE LEFT DARKLING.

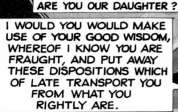

ARE YOU OUR DAUGHTER?

I WOULD YOU WOULD MAKE USE OF YOUR GOOD WISDOM, WHEREOF I KNOW YOU ARE FRAUGHT, AND PUT AWAY THESE DISPOSITIONS WHICH OF LATE TRANSPORT YOU FROM WHAT YOU RIGHTLY ARE.

MAY NOT AN ASS KNOW WHEN A CART DRAWS THE HORSE?

WHOOP, JUG!

I LOVE THEE!

DOES ANY HERE KNOW ME? THIS IS NOT LEAR! DOES LEAR WALK THUS? SPEAK THUS? WHERE ARE HIS EYES?

EITHER HIS NOTION WEAKENS, HIS DISCERNINGS ARE LETHARGIED —

HA! WAKING? 'TIS NOT SO!

WHO IS IT THAT CAN TELL ME WHO I AM?

LEAR'S SHADOW.

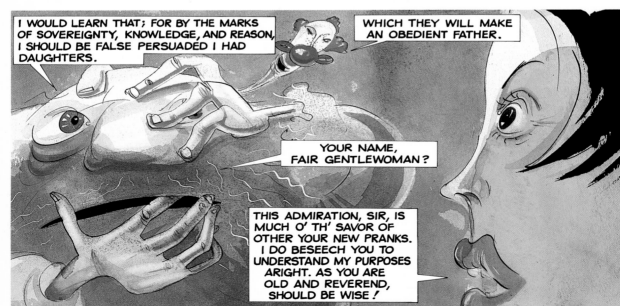

I WOULD LEARN THAT; FOR BY THE MARKS OF SOVEREIGNTY, KNOWLEDGE, AND REASON, I SHOULD BE FALSE PERSUADED I HAD DAUGHTERS.

WHICH THEY WILL MAKE AN OBEDIENT FATHER.

YOUR NAME, FAIR GENTLEWOMAN?

THIS ADMIRATION, SIR, IS MUCH O' TH' SAVOR OF OTHER YOUR NEW PRANKS. I DO BESEECH YOU TO UNDERSTAND MY PURPOSES ARIGHT. AS YOU ARE OLD AND REVEREND, SHOULD BE WISE!

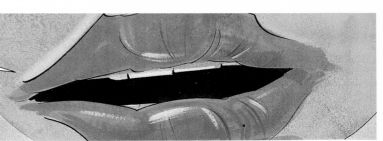

HERE DO YOU KEEP
A HUNDRED KNIGHTS AND SQUIRES;
MEN SO DISORDERED,
SO DEBOSHED AND BOLD,
THAT THIS OUR COURT,
INFECTED WITH THEIR MANNERS,
SHOWS LIKE A RIOTOUS INN;
EPICURISM AND LUST MAKES IT
MORE LIKE A TAVERN OR A BROTHEL
THAN A GRACED PALACE.

THE SHAME ITSELF DOTH SPEAK FOR INSTANT REMEDY;
BE THEN DESIRED BY HER (THAT ELSE WILL TAKE
THE THING SHE BEGS) A LITTLE TO DISQUANTITY
YOUR TRAIN; AND THE REMAINDERS, THAT SHALL STILL
DEPEND, TO BE SUCH MEN AS MAY BESORT YOUR AGE,
WHICH KNOW THEMSELVES AND YOU.

DARKNESS AND DEVILS!

SADDLE MY HORSES!
CALL MY TRAIN
TOGETHER!

DEGENERATE BASTARD!
I'LL NOT TROUBLE THEE;
YET HAVE I LEFT
A DAUGHTER.

YOU STRIKE
MY PEOPLE,
AND YOUR
DISORDERED RABBLE
MAKE SERVANTS
OF THEIR BETTERS.

WOE, THAT
TOO LATE
REPENTS.

ENTER ALBANY

O, SIR, ARE YOU COME?

IS IT
YOUR
WILL?

SPEAK, SIR!

PREPARE MY HORSES!

INGRATITUDE, THOU
MARBLE-HEARTED FIEND,
MORE HIDEOUS, WHEN THOU
SHOW'ST THEE IN A CHILD,
THAN THE SEA-MONSTER!

PRAY, SIR,
BE PATIENT.

DETESTED KITE, THOU LIEST! MY TRAIN ARE MEN OF CHOICE AND RAREST PARTS, THAT ALL PARTICULARS OF DUTY KNOW, AND IN THE MOST EXACT REGARD SUPPORT THE WORSHIPS OF THEIR NAME.

O MOST SMALL FAULT, HOW UGLY DIDST THOU IN CORDELIA SHOW! WHICH, LIKE AN ENGINE, WRENCHED MY FRAME OF NATURE FROM THE FIXÈD PLACE, DREW FROM MY HEART ALL LOVE, AND ADDED TO THE GALL.

O LEAR, LEAR, LEAR! BEAT AT THIS GATE THAT LET THY FOLLY IN, AND THY DEAR JUDGEMENT OUT! GO, GO, MY PEOPLE!

MY LORD, I AM GUILTLESS, AS I AM IGNORANT, OF WHAT HATH MOVED YOU.

IT MAY BE SO, MY LORD.

HEAR, NATURE, HEAR! DEAR GODDESS, HEAR! SUSPEND THY PURPOSE IF THOU DIDST INTEND TO MAKE THIS CREATURE FRUITFUL! INTO HER WOMB CONVEY STERILITY! DRY UP IN HER THE ORGANS OF INCREASE, AND FROM HER DEROGATE BODY NEVER SPRING A BABE TO HONOUR HER!

IF SHE MUST TEEM, CREATE HER CHILD OF SPLEEN THAT IT MAY LIVE TO BE A THWART DISNATURED TORMENT TO HER! LET IT STAMP WRINKLES IN HER BROW OF YOUTH, WITH CADENT TEARS FRET CHANNELS IN HER CHEEKS, TURN ALL HER MOTHER'S PAINS AND BENEFITS TO LAUGHTER AND CONTEMPT, THAT SHE MAY FEEL HOW SHARPER THAN A SERPENT'S TOOTH IT IS TO HAVE A THANKLESS CHILD!

AWAY, AWAY!

NOW GODS THAT WE ADORE, WHEREOF COMES THIS?

NEVER AFFLICT YOURSELF TO KNOW MORE OF IT: BUT LET HIS DISPOSITION HAVE THAT SCOPE AS DOTAGE GIVES IT.

WHAT! FIFTY OF MY FOLLOWERS. AT A CLAP — WITHIN A FORTNIGHT?

WHAT'S THE MATTER, SIR?

I'LL TELL THEE —

LIFE AND DEATH! I AM ASHAMED THAT THOU HAST POWER TO SHAKE MY MANHOOD THUS, THAT THESE HOT TEARS, WHICH BREAK FROM ME PERFORCE, SHOULD MAKE THEE WORTH THEM. BLASTS AND FOGS UPON THEE! TH'UNTENTED WOUNDINGS OF A FATHER'S CURSE PIERCE EVERY SENSE ABOUT THEE!

OLD FOND EYES, BEWEEP THIS CAUSE AGAIN; I'LL PLUCK YE OUT, AND CAST YOU, WITH THE WATERS THAT YOU LOOSE, TO TEMPER CLAY. YEA, IS'T COME TO THIS?

HA! LET IT BE SO: I HAVE ANOTHER DAUGHTER WHO, I AM SURE, IS KIND AND COMFORTABLE; WHEN SHE SHALL HEAR THIS OF THEE, WITH HER NAILS SHE'LL FLAY THY WOLVISH VISAGE.

THOU SHALT FIND THAT I'LL RESUME THE SHAPE WHICH THOU DOST THINK I HAVE CAST OFF FOREVER.

DO YOU MARK THAT?

I CANNOT BE SO PARTIAL, GONERIL, TO THE GREAT LOVE I BEAR YOU —

. PRAY YOU, CONTENT!

WHAT, OSWALD, HO!

YOU, SIR, MORE KNAVE THAN FOOL! AFTER YOUR MASTER!

NUNCLE LEAR, NUNCLE LEAR! TARRY, TAKE THE FOOL WITH THEE!

A FOX, WHEN ONE HAS CAUGHT HER, AND SUCH A DAUGHTER, SHOULD SURE TO THE SLAUGHTER, IF MY CAP WOULD BUY A HALTER. SO THE FOOL FOLLOWS AFTER.

THIS MAN HATH HAD GOOD COUNSEL! A HUNDRED KNIGHTS! 'TIS POLITIC AND SAFE TO LET HIM KEEP AT POINT A HUNDRED KNIGHTS! YES, THAT ON EVERY DREAM, EACH BUZZ, EACH FANCY, EACH COMPLAINT, DISLIKE, HE MAY ENGUARD HIS DOTAGE WITH THEIR POWERS, AND HOLD OUR LIVES IN MERCY!

OSWALD, I SAY!

WELL, YOU MAY FEAR TOO FAR.

SAFER THAN TRUST TOO FAR.

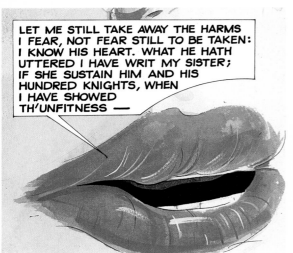

LET ME STILL TAKE AWAY THE HARMS I FEAR, NOT FEAR STILL TO BE TAKEN: I KNOW HIS HEART. WHAT HE HATH UTTERED I HAVE WRIT MY SISTER; IF SHE SUSTAIN HIM AND HIS HUNDRED KNIGHTS, WHEN I HAVE SHOWED TH'UNFITNESS —

HOW NOW, OSWALD! WHAT, HAVE YOU WRIT THAT LETTER TO MY SISTER?

AY, MADAM.

TAKE YOU SOME COMPANY, AND AWAY TO HORSE. INFORM HER FULL OF MY PARTICULAR FEAR; AND THERETO ADD SUCH REASONS OF YOU OWN AS MAY COMPACT IT MORE. GET YOU GONE, AND HASTEN YOUR RETURN.

NO, NO, MY LORD; THIS MILKY GENTLENESS AND COURSE OF YOURS THOUGH I CONDEMN NOT, YET (UNDER PARDON) YOU ARE MUCH MORE A-TAXED FOR WANT OF WISDOM THAN PRAISED FOR HARMFUL MILDNESS.

HOW FAR YOUR EYES MAY PIERCE I CANNOT TELL: STRIVING TO BETTER, OFT WE, MAR WHAT'S WELL.

NAY, THEN—

WELL, WELL; TH'EVENT.

GO YOU BEFORE TO GLOUCESTER WITH THESE LETTERS. ACQUAINT MY DAUGHTER NO FURTHER WITH ANYTHING YOU KNOW THAN COMES FROM HER DEMAND OUT OF THE LETTER.

IF YOUR DILIGENCE BE NOT SPEEDY, I SHALL BE THERE AFORE YOU.

I WILL NOT SLEEP, MY LORD, TILL I HAVE DELIVERED YOUR LETTER.

IF A MAN'S BRAINS WERE IN'S HEELS, WERE'T NOT IN DANGER OF KIBES?

AY, BOY.

THEN, I PRITHEE, BE MERRY; THY WIT SHALL NOT GO SLIPSHOD.

HA, HA, HA!

SHALT SEE THY OTHER DAUGHTER WILL USE THEE KINDLY; FOR THOUGH SHE'S AS LIKE THIS AS A CRAB'S LIKE AN APPLE,

YET I CAN TELL WHAT I CAN TELL.

WHAT CANST TELL, BOY?

SHE WILL TASTE AS LIKE THIS AS A CRAB DOES TO A CRAB.

CANST THOU TELL WHY ONE'S NOSE

STANDS I'TH'MIDDLE ON'S FACE?

NO.

WHY, TO KEEP ONE'S EYES OF EITHER SIDE'S NOSE;

THAT WHAT A MAN CANNOT SMELL OUT, HE MAY SPY INTO.

I DID HER WRONG!

CANST TELL HOW AN OYSTER MAKES HIS SHELL?

NO.

NOR I NEITHER.

BUT I CAN TELL WHY A SNAIL HAS A HOUSE.

WHY?

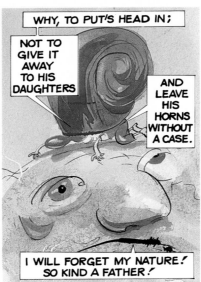

WHY, TO PUT'S HEAD IN; NOT TO GIVE IT AWAY TO HIS DAUGHTERS

AND LEAVE HIS HORNS WITHOUT A CASE.

I WILL FORGET MY NATURE! SO KIND A FATHER!

BE MY HORSES READY?

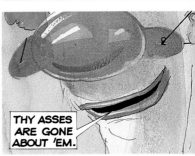

THY ASSES ARE GONE ABOUT 'EM.

THE REASON WHY THE SEVEN STARS ARE NO MO THAN SEVEN IS A PRETTY REASON.

BECAUSE THEY ARE NOT EIGHT?

YES, INDEED!

THOU WOULD'ST MAKE A GOOD FOOL!

TO TAKE'T AGAIN PERFORCE! MONSTER INGRATITUDE!

IF THOU WERT MY FOOL, NUNCLE, I'D HAVE THEE BEATEN FOR BEING OLD BEFORE THY TIME.

HOW'S THAT?

THOU SHOULD'ST NOT HAVE BEEN OLD TILL THOU HADST BEEN WISE.

O! LET ME NOT BE MAD, NOT MAD, SWEET HEAVEN!

KEEP ME IN TEMPER: I WOULD NOT BE MAD!

HOW NOW, ARE THE HORSES READY?

READY, MY LORD.

COME, BOY.

SHE THAT'S A MAID NOW, AND LAUGHS AT MY DEPARTURE, SHALL NOT BE A MAID LONG — UNLESS THINGS BE CUT SHORTER.

SAVE THEE, CURAN.

AND YOU, SIR.

I HAVE BEEN WITH YOUR FATHER, AND GIVEN HIM NOTICE THAT THE DUKE OF CORNWALL AND REGAN HIS DUCHESS WILL BE HERE WITH HIM THIS NIGHT.

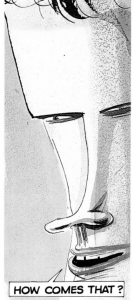

HOW COMES THAT?

NAY, I KNOW NOT. YOU HAVE HEARD OF THE NEWS ABROAD?

I MEAN THE WHISPERED ONES, FOR THEY ARE YET BUT EAR-BUSSING ARGUMENTS.

NOT I. PRAY YOU, WHAT ARE THEY?

HAVE YOU HEARD OF NO LIKELY WARS TOWARD, 'TWIXT THE DUKES OF CORNWALL AND ALBANY?

NOT A WORD.

YOU MAY DO, THEN, IN TIME.

FARE YOU WELL, SIR.

THE DUKE BE HERE TONIGHT?

THE BETTER! BEST!

THIS WEAVES ITSELF PERFORCE INTO MY BUSINESS.

MY FATHER HATH SET GUARD TO TAKE MY BROTHER.

AND I HAVE ONE THING OF A QUEASY QUESTION WHICH I MUST ACT.

BRIEFNESS AND FORTUNE, WORK!

BROTHER, A WORD! DESCEND, BROTHER, I SAY!

MY FATHER WATCHES: O, SIR, FLY THIS PLACE!

INTELLIGENCE IS GIVEN WHERE YOU ARE HID!

YOU HAVE NOW THE GOOD ADVANTAGE OF THE NIGHT.

HAVE YOU NOT SPOKEN 'GAINST THE DUKE OF CORNWALL? HE'S COMING HITHER NOW, I' TH' NIGHT, I' TH' HASTE, AND REGAN WITH HIM.

HAVE YOU NOTHING SAID UPON HIS PARTY 'GAINST THE DUKE OF ALBANY?

ADVISE YOURSELF.

I AM SURE ON'T: NOT A WORD.

I HEAR MY FATHER COMING; PARDON ME, IN CUNNING I MUST DRAW MY SWORD UPON YOU.

DRAW: SEEM TO DEFEND YOURSELF.

NOW QUIT YOU WELL.

YIELD! COME BEFORE MY FATHER!

LIGHT, HO! HERE!

FLY, BROTHER.

TORCHES! TORCHES!

SO, FAREWELL.

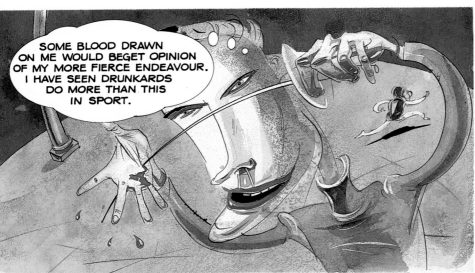

SOME BLOOD DRAWN ON ME WOULD BEGET OPINION OF MY MORE FIERCE ENDEAVOUR. I HAVE SEEN DRUNKARDS DO MORE THAN THIS IN SPORT.

FATHER! FATHER!

STOP! STOP!

NO HELP?

NOW, EDMUND, WHERE'S THE VILLAIN?

HERE STOOD HE IN THE DARK, HIS SHARP SWORD OUT, MUMBLING OF WICKED CHARMS, CONJURING THE MOON TO STAND AUSPICIOUS MISTRESS —

BUT WHERE IS HE?

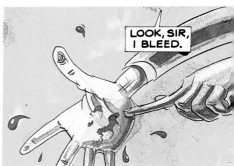

LOOK, SIR, I BLEED.

WHERE IS THE VILLAIN, EDMUND?

FLED THIS WAY, SIR, WHEN BY NO MEANS HE COULD —

PURSUE HIM, HO! GO AFTER!

BY NO MEANS WHAT?

PERSUADE ME TO THE MURDER OF YOUR LORDSHIP; BUT THAT I TOLD HIM THE REVENGING GODS 'GAINST PARRICIDES DID ALL THEIR THUNDERS BEND; SPOKE WITH HOW MANIFOLD AND STRONG A BOND THE CHILD WAS BOUND TO TH' FATHER.

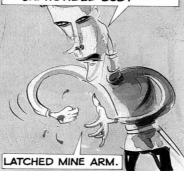

SIR, IN FINE, SEEING HOW LOATHLY OPPOSITE I STOOD TO HIS UNNATURAL PURPOSE, IN FELL MOTION, WITH HIS PREPARÈD SWORD, HE CHARGES HOME MY UNPROVIDED BODY —

LATCHED MINE ARM.

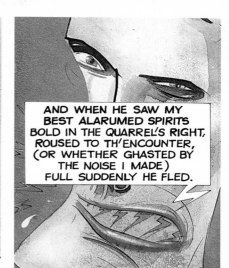

AND WHEN HE SAW MY BEST ALARUMED SPIRITS BOLD IN THE QUARREL'S RIGHT, ROUSED TO TH' ENCOUNTER, (OR WHETHER GHASTED BY THE NOISE I MADE) FULL SUDDENLY HE FLED.

LET HIM FLY FAR: NOT IN THIS LAND SHALL HE REMAIN UNCAUGHT!

AND FOUND — DISPATCH!

THE NOBLE DUKE, MY MASTER, MY WORTHY ARCH AND PATRON, COMES TONIGHT.

BY HIS AUTHORITY I WILL PROCLAIM IT:

THAT HE WHICH FINDS HIM SHALL DESERVE OUR THANKS, BRINGING THE MURDEROUS COWARD TO THE STAKE; HE THAT CONCEALS HIM — DEATH!

WHEN I DISSUADED HIM FROM HIS INTENT, AND FOUND HIM PIGHT TO DO IT, WITH CURST SPEECH I THREATENED TO DISCOVER HIM.

HE REPLIED: "THOU UNPOSSESSING BASTARD!"

"DOST THOU THINK, IF I WOULD STAND AGAINST THEE, WOULD THE REPOSAL OF ANY TRUST, VIRTUE OR WORTH IN THEE MAKE THY WORDS FAITHED?"

"NO! WHAT I SHOULD DENY (AS THIS I WOULD — AY, THOUGH THOU DIDST PRODUCE MY VERY CHARACTER) I'D TURN IT ALL TO THY SUGGESTION, PLOT AND DAMNÈD PRACTICE."

"AND THOU MUST MAKE A DULLARD OF THE WORLD, IF THEY NOT THOUGHT THE PROFITS OF MY DEATH WERE VERY PREGNANT AND POTENTIAL SPURS TO MAKE THEE SEEK IT."

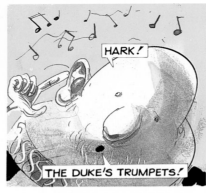

EDMUND, I HEAR THAT YOU HAVE SHOWN YOUR FATHER A CHILD-LIKE OFFICE.

IT WAS MY DUTY, SIR.

HE DID BEWRAY HIS PRACTICE; AND RECEIVED THIS HURT YOU SEE, STRIVING TO APPREHEND HIM.

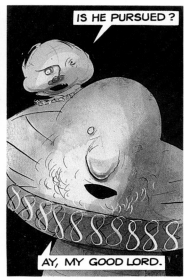

IS HE PURSUED?

AY, MY GOOD LORD.

IF HE BE TAKEN, HE SHALL NEVER MORE BE FEARED OF DOING HARM; MAKE YOUR OWN PURPOSE, HOW IN MY STRENGTH YOU PLEASE.

FOR YOU, EDMUND, WHOSE VIRTUE AND OBEDIENCE DOTH THIS INSTANT SO MUCH COMMEND ITSELF, YOU SHALL BE OURS.

NATURES OF SUCH DEEP TRUST WE SHALL MUCH NEED; YOU WE FIRST SEIZE ON.

I SHALL SERVE YOU, SIR — TRULY, HOWEVER ELSE.

FOR HIM I THANK YOUR GRACE.

YOU KNOW NOT WHY WE CAME TO VISIT YOU —

—THUS OUT OF SEASON, THREADING DARK-EYED NIGHT: OCCASIONS, NOBLE GLOUCESTER, OF SOME PRIZE, WHEREIN WE MUST HAVE USE OF YOUR ADVICE.

OUR FATHER HE HATH WRIT, SO HATH OUR SISTER, OF DIFFERENCES, WHICH I BEST THOUGHT IT FIT TO ANSWER FROM OUR HOME.

THE SEVERAL MESSENGERS FROM HENCE ATTEND DISPATCH.

OUR GOOD OLD FRIEND. LAY COMFORTS TO YOUR BOSOM, AND BESTOW YOUR NEEDFUL COUNSEL TO OUR BUSINESSES, WHICH CRAVES THE INSTANT USE.

I SERVE YOU, MADAM.

YOUR GRACES ARE RIGHT WELCOME.

43

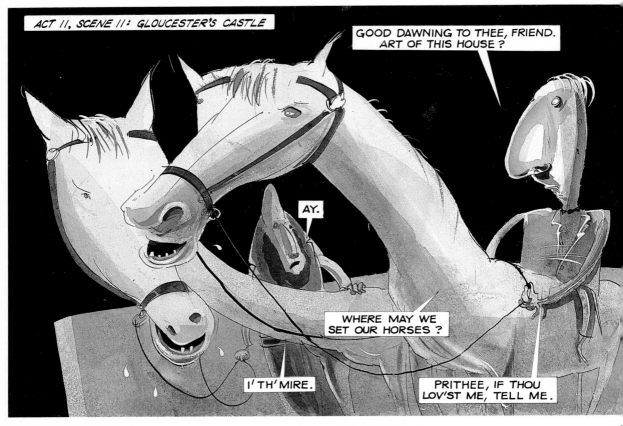

ACT II, SCENE II: GLOUCESTER'S CASTLE

GOOD DAWNING TO THEE, FRIEND. ART OF THIS HOUSE?

AY.

WHERE MAY WE SET OUR HORSES?

I' TH' MIRE.

PRITHEE, IF THOU LOV'ST ME, TELL ME.

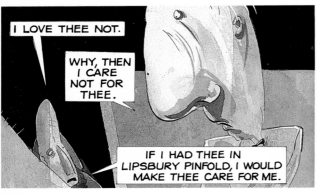

I LOVE THEE NOT.

WHY, THEN I CARE NOT FOR THEE.

IF I HAD THEE IN LIPSBURY PINFOLD, I WOULD MAKE THEE CARE FOR ME.

WHY DOST THOU USE ME THUS? I KNOW THEE NOT.

FELLOW, I KNOW THEE!

WHAT DOST THOU KNOW ME FOR?

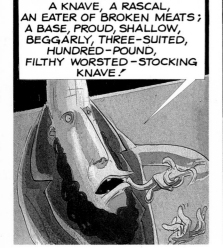

A KNAVE, A RASCAL, AN EATER OF BROKEN MEATS; A BASE, PROUD, SHALLOW, BEGGARLY, THREE-SUITED, HUNDRED-POUND, FILTHY WORSTED-STOCKING KNAVE!

A LILY-LIVERED, ACTION-TAKING, WHORESON, GLASS-GAZING, SUPER-SERVICEABLE, FINICAL ROGUE; ONE-TRUNK-INHERITING SLAVE; ONE THAT WOULDST BE A BAWD, IN WAY OF GOOD SERVICE, AND ART NOTHING BUT THE COMPOSITION OF A KNAVE, BEGGAR, COWARD, PANDER—

AND THE SON AND HEIR OF A MONGREL BITCH!

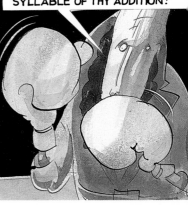

ONE WHOM I WILL BEAT INTO CLAMOROUS WHINING IF THOU DENI'ST THE LEAST SYLLABLE OF THY ADDITION!

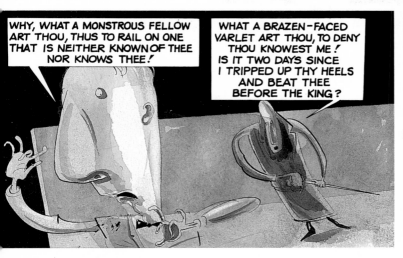

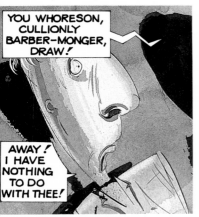

KEEP PEACE, UPON YOUR LIVES:
HE DIES THAT STRIKES AGAIN!
WHAT IS THE MATTER?

THE MESSENGERS
FROM OUR SISTER
AND THE KING.

WHAT IS YOUR
DIFFERENCE?
SPEAK!

I AM SCARCE
IN BREATH,
MY LORD.

NO MARVEL, YOU
HAVE SO BESTIRRED
YOUR VALOUR.
YOU COWARDLY
RASCAL, NATURE
DISCLAIMS IN THEE:
A TAILOR
MADE THEE.

THOU ART A
STRANGE FELLOW;
A TAILOR MAKE
A MAN?

A TAILOR, SIR:
A STONE CUTTER OR
A PAINTER COULD NOT
HAVE MADE HIM SO ILL,
THOUGH THEY HAD BEEN
BUT TWO YEARS O'TH'TRADE.

SPEAK YET: HOW GREW YOUR QUARREL?

THIS ANCIENT
RUFFIAN, SIR,
WHOSE LIFE
I HAVE SPARED
AT SUIT OF HIS
GREY BEARD—

THOU WHORESON ZED!
THOU UNNECESSARY LETTER!

MY LORD,
IF YOU WILL GIVE ME LEAVE,
I WILL TREAD THIS UNBOLTED
VILLAIN INTO MORTAR, AND DAUB
THE WALLS OF A JAKES WITH HIM.

SPARE MY
GREY BEARD,
YOU
WAGTAIL?

PEACE, SIRRAH!
YOU BEASTLY KNAVE,
KNOW YOU NO
REVERENCE?

YES, SIR;
BUT ANGER HATH
A PRIVILEGE.

WHY ART THOU ANGRY?

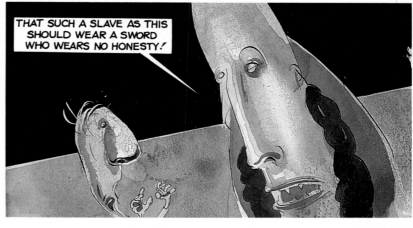

THAT SUCH A SLAVE AS THIS SHOULD WEAR A SWORD WHO WEARS NO HONESTY!

SUCH SMILING ROGUES AS THESE, LIKE RATS, OFT BITE THE HOLY CORDS ATWAIN WHICH ARE TOO INTRINCE T'UNLOOSE; SMOOTH EVERY PASSION THAT IN THE NATURES OF THEIR LORDS REBEL;

BRING OIL TO FIRE, SNOW TO THEIR COLDER MOODS; RENEGE, AFFIRM, AND TURN THEIR HALCYON BEAKS WITH EVERY GALE AND VARY OF THEIR MASTERS, KNOWING NOUGHT, LIKE DOGS, BUT FOLLOWING.

A PLAGUE UPON YOUR EPILEPTIC VISAGE! SMOILE YOU MY SPEECHES, AS I WERE A FOOL?

GOOSE, IF I HAD YOU UPON SARUM PLAIN, I'D DRIVE YE CACKLING HOME TO CAMELOT!

WHAT! ART THOU MAD, OLD FELLOW?

HOW FELL YOU OUT? SAY THAT.

NO CONTRARIES HOLD MORE ANTIPATHY THAN I AND SUCH A KNAVE.

WHY DOST THOU CALL HIM KNAVE? WHAT IS HIS FAULT?

HIS COUNTENANCE LIKES ME NOT.

NO MORE, PERCHANCE, DOES MINE, NOR HIS, NOR HERS.

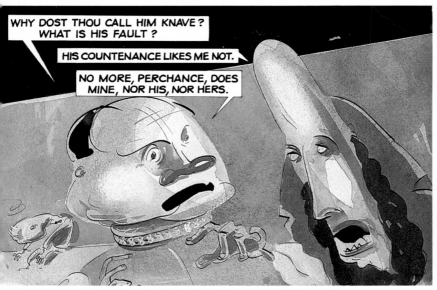

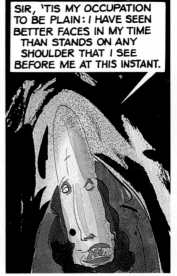

SIR, 'TIS MY OCCUPATION TO BE PLAIN: I HAVE SEEN BETTER FACES IN MY TIME THAN STANDS ON ANY SHOULDER THAT I SEE BEFORE ME AT THIS INSTANT.

THIS IS SOME FELLOW WHO, HAVING BEEN PRAISED FOR BLUNTNESS, DOTH AFFECT A SAUCY ROUGHNESS, AND CONSTRAINS THE GARB QUITE FROM HIS NATURE.

HE CANNOT FLATTER, HE! AN HONEST MIND, AND PLAIN! HE MUST SPEAK TRUTH.

AND THEY WILL TAKE IT, SO; IF NOT, HE'S PLAIN.

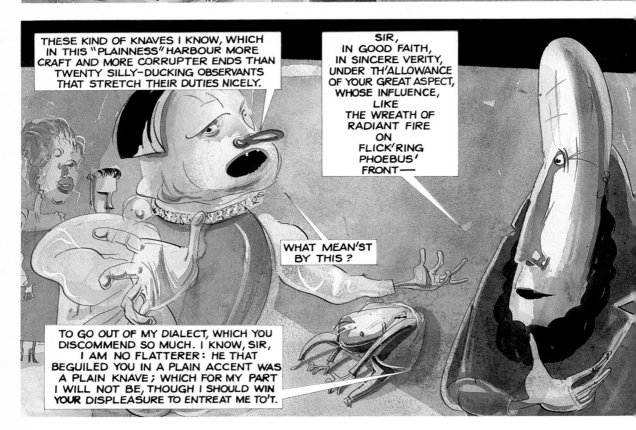

THESE KIND OF KNAVES I KNOW, WHICH IN THIS "PLAINNESS" HARBOUR MORE CRAFT AND MORE CORRUPTER ENDS THAN TWENTY SILLY-DUCKING OBSERVANTS THAT STRETCH THEIR DUTIES NICELY.

SIR, IN GOOD FAITH, IN SINCERE VERITY, UNDER TH'ALLOWANCE OF YOUR GREAT ASPECT, WHOSE INFLUENCE, LIKE THE WREATH OF RADIANT FIRE ON FLICK'RING PHOEBUS' FRONT—

WHAT MEAN'ST BY THIS?

TO GO OUT OF MY DIALECT, WHICH YOU DISCOMMEND SO MUCH. I KNOW, SIR, I AM NO FLATTERER: HE THAT BEGUILED YOU IN A PLAIN ACCENT WAS A PLAIN KNAVE; WHICH FOR MY PART I WILL NOT BE, THOUGH I SHOULD WIN YOUR DISPLEASURE TO ENTREAT ME TO'T.

WHAT WAS TH'OFFENCE YOU GAVE HIM?

I NEVER GAVE HIM ANY; IT PLEASED THE KING HIS MASTER VERY LATE TO STRIKE AT ME, UPON HIS MISCONSTRUCTION; WHEN HE, COMPACT, AND FLATTERING HIS DISPLEASURE, TRIPPED ME BEHIND; BEING DOWN, INSULTED, RAILED, AND PUT UPON HIM SUCH A DEAL OF MAN THAT WORTHIED HIM, GOT PRAISES OF THE KING FOR HIM ATTEMPTING WHO WAS SELF-SUBDUED; AND, IN THE FLESHMENT OF THIS DREAD EXPLOIT, DREW ON ME HERE AGAIN.

NONE OF THESE ROGUES AND COWARDS BUT AJAX IS THEIR FOOL.

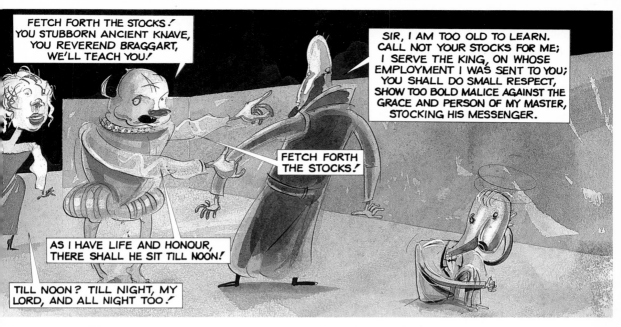

MY SISTER MAY RECEIVE IT MUCH MORE WORSE, TO HAVE HER GENTLEMAN ABUSED, ASSAULTED FOR FOLLOWING HER AFFAIRS.

PUT IN HIS LEGS!

COME, MY GOOD LORD, AWAY.

I AM SORRY FOR THEE, FRIEND; 'TIS THE DUKE'S PLEASURE, WHOSE DISPOSITION, ALL THE WORLD WELL KNOWS, WILL NOT BE RUBBED NOR STOPPED.

I'LL ENTREAT FOR THEE.

PRAY DO NOT, SIR. I HAVE WATCHED AND TRAVELLED HARD; SOME TIME I SHALL SLEEP OUT, THE REST I'LL WHISTLE.

A GOOD MAN'S FORTUNE MAY GROW OUT AT HEELS.

GIVE YOU GOOD MORROW.

THE DUKE'S TO BLAME IN THIS; 'TWILL BE ILL TAKEN.

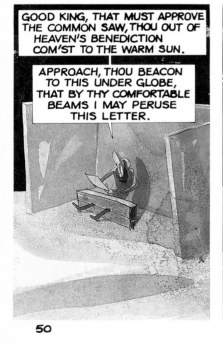

GOOD KING, THAT MUST APPROVE THE COMMON SAW, THOU OUT OF HEAVEN'S BENEDICTION COM'ST TO THE WARM SUN.

APPROACH, THOU BEACON TO THIS UNDER GLOBE, THAT BY THY COMFORTABLE BEAMS I MAY PERUSE THIS LETTER.

NOTHING ALMOST SEES MIRACLES BUT MISERY: I KNOW 'TIS FROM CORDELIA, WHO HATH MOST FORTUNATELY BEEN INFORMED OF MY OBSCURÈD COURSE; AND SHALL FIND TIME, FROM THIS ENORMOUS STATE, SEEKING TO GIVE LOSSES THEIR REMEDIES.

ALL WEARY AND O'ERWATCHED, TAKE VANTAGE, HEAVY EYES, NOT TO BEHOLD THIS SHAMEFUL LODGING.

FORTUNE, GOOD NIGHT; SMILE ONCE MORE; TURN THY WHEEL!

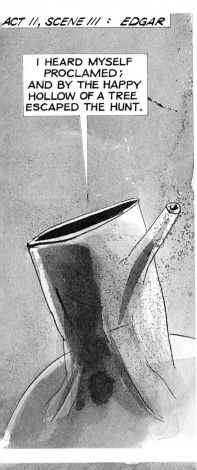

I HEARD MYSELF PROCLAMED; AND BY THE HAPPY HOLLOW OF A TREE ESCAPED THE HUNT.

NO PORT IS FREE; NO PLACE THAT GUARD AND MOST UNUSUAL VIGILANCE DOES NOT ATTEND MY TAKING.

WHILES I MAY 'SCAPE, I WILL PRESERVE MYSELF; AND AM BETHOUGHT TO TAKE THE BASEST AND MOST POOREST SHAPE THAT EVER PENURY, IN CONTEMPT OF MAN, BROUGHT NEAR TO BEAST.

MY FACE I'LL GRIME WITH FILTH, BLANKET MY LOINS, ELF ALL MY HAIR IN KNOTS,

AND WITH PRESENTED NAKEDNESS OUTFACE THE WINDS AND PERSECUTIONS OF THE SKY.

THE COUNTRY GIVES ME PROOF AND PRECEDENT OF BEDLAM BEGGARS WHO, WITH ROARING VOICES, STRIKE IN THEIR NUMBED AND MORTIFIED BARE ARMS PINS, WOODEN PRICKS, NAILS, SPRIGS OF ROSEMARY,

AND WITH THIS HORRIBLE OBJECT, FROM LOW FARMS, POOR PELTING VILLAGES, SHEEP-COTES AND MILLS, SOMETIME WITH LUNATIC BANS, SOMETIME WITH PRAYERS, ENFORCE THEIR CHARITY.

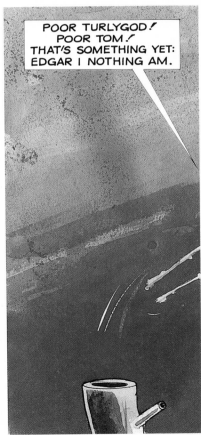

POOR TURLYGOD! POOR TOM! THAT'S SOMETHING YET: EDGAR I NOTHING AM.

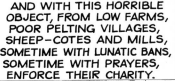

'TIS STRANGE THAT THEY SHOULD SO DEPART FROM HOME, AND NOT SEND BACK MY MESSENGER.

AS I LEARNED, THE NIGHT BEFORE THERE WAS NO PURPOSE IN THEM OF THIS REMOVE.

HAIL TO THEE, NOBLE MASTER!

HA! MAK'ST THOU THIS SHAME THY PASTIME?

NO, MY LORD.

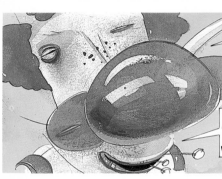

HA, HA! HE WEARS CRUEL GARTERS. HORSES ARE TIED BY THE HEADS, DOGS AND BEARS BY TH'NECK, MONKEYS BY TH'LOINS, AND MEN BY TH'LEGS.

WHEN A MAN'S OVER-LUSTY AT LEGS, THEN HE WEARS WOODEN NETHER-STOCKS.

WHAT'S HE THAT HATH SO MUCH THY PLACE MISTOOK TO SET THEE HERE?

IT IS BOTH HE AND SHE; YOUR SON AND DAUGHTER.

NO.

YES.

NO, I SAY.

I SAY YEA.

NO, NO; THEY WOULD NOT!

YES, YES; THEY HAVE!

BY JUPITER, I SWEAR NO!

BY JUNO, I SWEAR AY!

THEY DURST NOT DO'T; THEY COULD NOT, WOULD NOT DO'T; 'TIS WORSE THAN MURDER, TO DO UPON RESPECT SUCH VIOLENT OUTRAGE. RESOLVE ME, WITH ALL MODEST HASTE, WHICH WAY THOU MIGHT'ST DESERVE, OR THEY IMPOSE, THIS USAGE, COMING FROM US.

MY LORD, WHEN AT THEIR HOME I DID COMMEND YOUR HIGHNESS' LETTERS TO THEM, ERE I WAS RISEN FROM THE PLACE THAT SHOWED MY DUTY KNEELING,

CAME THERE A REEKING POST, STEWED IN HIS HASTE, HALF BREATHLESS, PANTING FORTH FROM GONERIL HIS MISTRESS SALUTATIONS;

DELIVERED LETTERS, SPITE OF INTERMISSION, WHICH PRESENTLY THEY READ: ON WHOSE CONTENTS THEY SUMMONED UP THEIR MEINY, STRAIGHT TOOK HORSE; COMMANDED ME TO FOLLOW,

AND ATTEND THE LEISURE OF THEIR ANSWER; GAVE ME COLD LOOKS. AND MEETING HERE THE OTHER MESSENGER, WHOSE WELCOME, I PERCEIVED, HAD POISONED MINE —

BEING THE VERY FELLOW WHICH OF LATE DISPLAYED SO SAUCILY AGAINST YOUR HIGHNESS — HAVING MORE MAN THAN WIT ABOUT ME, DREW. HE RAISED THE HOUSE WITH LOUD AND COWARD CRIES.

YOUR SON AND DAUGHTER FOUND THIS TRESPASS WORTH THE SHAME WHICH HERE IT SUFFERS.

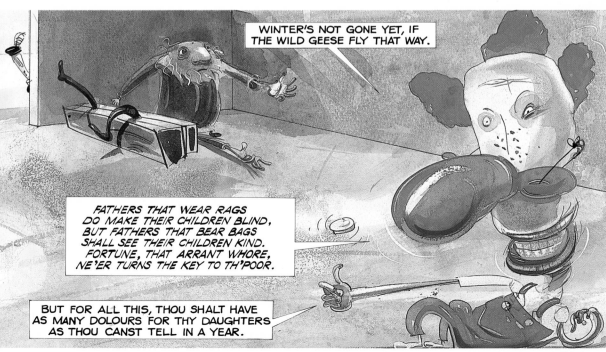

WINTER'S NOT GONE YET, IF THE WILD GEESE FLY THAT WAY.

FATHERS THAT WEAR RAGS DO MAKE THEIR CHILDREN BLIND, BUT FATHERS THAT BEAR BAGS SHALL SEE THEIR CHILDREN KIND. FORTUNE, THAT ARRANT WHORE, NE'ER TURNS THE KEY TO TH'POOR.

BUT FOR ALL THIS, THOU SHALT HAVE AS MANY DOLOURS FOR THY DAUGHTERS AS THOU CANST TELL IN A YEAR.

THAT SIR WHICH SERVES
AND SEEKS FOR GAIN,
AND FOLLOWS BUT FOR FORM,
WILL PACK WHEN IT
BEGINS TO RAIN,
AND LEAVE THEE IN THE STORM.
BUT I WILL TARRY,
THE FOOL WILL STAY,
AND LET THE WISE MAN FLY:
THE KNAVE TURNS FOOL
THAT RUNS AWAY;
THE FOOL NO KNAVE, PERDY.

WHERE LEARNED YOU THIS, FOOL?

NOT I'TH'STOCKS, FOOL.

DENY TO SPEAK WITH ME?
THEY ARE SICK?
THEY ARE WEARY?
THEY HAVE TRAVELLED
ALL THE NIGHT?
MERE FETCHES!
AY, THE IMAGES OF
REVOLT AND FLYING OFF!

FETCH ME A BETTER ANSWER!

MY DEAR LORD, YOU KNOW THE FIERY QUALITY OF THE DUKE; HOW UNREMOVABLE AND FIXED HE IS IN HIS OWN COURSE.

VENGEANCE! PLAGUE! DEATH! CONFUSION!

"FIERY"?

WHAT "QUALITY"?

WHY, GLOUCESTER, GLOUCESTER, I'D SPEAK WITH THE DUKE OF CORNWALL AND HIS WIFE!

WELL, MY GOOD LORD, I HAVE INFORMED THEM SO.

INFORMED THEM!

DOST THOU UNDERSTAND ME MAN?

AY, MY GOOD LORD.

THE KING WOULD SPEAK WITH CORNWALL!

THE DEAR FATHER WOULD WITH HIS DAUGHTER SPEAK!

COMMANDS, 'TENDS SERVICE!

ARE THEY "INFORMED" OF THIS?

MY BREATH AND BLOOD!

FIERY? THE FIERY DUKE?

TELL THE HOT DUKE THAT —

NO, BUT NOT YET!

MAYBE HE IS NOT WELL!

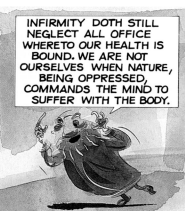

INFIRMITY DOTH STILL NEGLECT ALL OFFICE WHERETO OUR HEALTH IS BOUND. WE ARE NOT OURSELVES WHEN NATURE, BEING OPPRESSED, COMMANDS THE MIND TO SUFFER WITH THE BODY.

I'LL FORBEAR; AND AM FALL'N OUT WITH MY MORE HEADIER WILL, TO TAKE THE INDISPOSED AND SICKLY FIT FOR THE SOUND MAN.

DEATH ON MY STATE!

WHEREFORE SHOULD HE SIT THERE?

THIS ACT PERSUADES ME THAT THIS REMOTION OF THE DUKE AND HER IS PRACTICE ONLY.

GIVE ME MY SERVANT FORTH!

GO, TELL THE DUKE AND'S WIFE I'D SPEAK WITH THEM.

NOW! PRESENTLY!

BID THEM COME FORTH AND HEAR ME, OR AT THEIR CHAMBER-DOOR I'LL BEAT THE DRUM TILL IT CRY SLEEP TO DEATH!

I WOULD HAVE ALL WELL BETWIXT YOU.

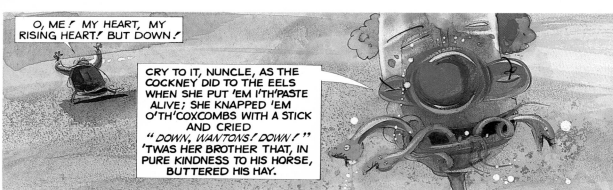

O, ME! MY HEART, MY RISING HEART! BUT DOWN!

CRY TO IT, NUNCLE, AS THE COCKNEY DID TO THE EELS WHEN SHE PUT 'EM I'TH'PASTE ALIVE; SHE KNAPPED 'EM O'TH'COXCOMBS WITH A STICK AND CRIED "DOWN, WANTONS! DOWN!" 'TWAS HER BROTHER THAT, IN PURE KINDNESS TO HIS HORSE, BUTTERED HIS HAY.

GOOD MORROW
TO YOU BOTH.

HAIL TO
YOUR GRACE.

I AM GLAD TO SEE
YOUR HIGHNESS.

REGAN, I THINK YOU ARE. I KNOW
WHAT REASON I HAVE TO THINK SO;
IF THOU SHOULDST NOT BE GLAD,
I WOULD DIVORCE ME FROM
THY MOTHER'S TOMB,
SEPULCHRING AN ADULTRESS.

O! ARE YOU FREE?

SOME OTHER TIME FOR THAT.

BELOVÈD REGAN,
THY SISTER'S NAUGHT.
O REGAN! SHE HATH TIED
SHARP-TOOTHED UNKINDNESS,
LIKE A VULTURE,

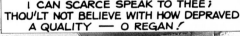

HERE.

I CAN SCARCE SPEAK TO THEE;
THOU'LT NOT BELIEVE WITH HOW DEPRAVED
A QUALITY — O REGAN!

I PRAY YOU, SIR, TAKE
PATIENCE. I HAVE HOPE
YOU LESS KNOW HOW
TO VALUE HER DESERT
THAN SHE TO SCANT
HER DUTY.

SAY?
HOW IS THAT?

I CANNOT THINK MY SISTER
IN THE LEAST WOULD FAIL
HER OBLIGATION.

IF, SIR, PERCHANCE
SHE HAVE RESTRANED
THE RIOTS OF YOUR
FOLLOWERS, 'TIS
ON SUCH GROUND, AND
TO SUCH WHOLESOME END,
AS CLEARS HER FROM
ALL BLAME.

MY CURSES ON HER!

O, SIR! YOU ARE OLD; NATURE IN YOU STANDS ON THE VERY VERGE OF HER CONFINE: YOU SHOULD BE RULED AND LED BY SOME DISCRETION THAT DISCERNS YOUR STATE BETTER THAN YOU YOURSELF. THEREFORE I PRAY YOU THAT TO OUR SISTER YOU DO MAKE RETURN; SAY YOU HAVE WRONGED HER.

ASK HER FORGIVENESS? DO YOU BUT MARK HOW THIS BECOMES THE HOUSE:

"DEAR DAUGHTER, I CONFESS THAT I AM OLD; AGE IS UNNECESSARY: ON MY KNEES I BEG THAT YOU'LL VOUCHSAFE ME RAIMENT, BED AND FOOD."

GOOD SIR, NO MORE; THESE ARE UNSIGHTLY TRICKS. RETURN YOU TO MY SISTER.

NEVER, REGAN. SHE HATH ABATED ME OF HALF MY TRAIN; LOOKED BLACK UPON ME; STRUCK ME WITH HER TONGUE, MOST SERPENT-LIKE, UPON THE VERY HEART.

ALL THE STORED VENGEANCES OF HEAVEN FALL ON HER INGRATEFUL TOP! STRIKE HER YOUNG BONES, YOU TAKING AIRS, WITH LAMENESS!

FIE, SIR, FIE!

YOU NIMBLE LIGHTNINGS, DART YOUR BLINDING FLAMES INTO HER SCORNFUL EYES!

INFECT HER BEAUTY, YOU FEN-SUCKED FOGS, DRAWN BY THE POW'RFUL SUN, TO FALL AND BLISTER HER!

O THE BLEST GODS! SO WILL YOU WISH ON ME, WHEN THE RASH MOOD IS ON.

NO, REGAN, THOU SHALT NEVER HAVE MY CURSE. THY TENDER-HEFTED NATURE SHALL NOT GIVE THEE O'ER TO HARSHNESS: HER EYES ARE FIERCE, BUT THINE DO COMFORT AND NOT BURN.

'TIS NOT IN THEE TO GRUDGE MY PLEASURES, TO CUT OFF MY TRAIN, TO BANDY HASTY WORDS, TO SCANT MY SIZES, AND IN CONCLUSION TO OPPOSE THE BOLT AGAINST MY COMING IN.

THOU BETTER KNOW'ST THE OFFICES OF NATURE, BOND OF CHILDHOOD, EFFECTS OF COURTESY, DUES OF GRATITUDE;

THY HALF O'TH'KINGDOM HAST THOU NOT FORGOT, WHEREIN I THEE ENDOWED.

59

O SIDES, YOU ARE TOO TOUGH! WILL YOU YET HOLD?

HOW CAME MY MAN I'TH'STOCKS?

I SET HIM THERE, SIR; BUT HIS OWN DISORDERS DESERVED MUCH LESS ADVANCEMENT.

YOU! DID YOU?

I PRAY YOU, FATHER, BEING WEAK, SEEM SO.

IF, TILL THE EXPIRATION OF YOUR MONTH, YOU WILL RETURN AND SOJOURN WITH MY SISTER, DISMISSING HALF YOUR TRAIN, COME THEN TO ME: I AM NOW FROM HOME, AND OUT OF THAT PROVISION WHICH SHALL BE NEEDFUL FOR YOUR ENTERTMENT.

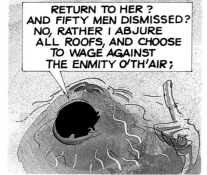

RETURN TO HER? AND FIFTY MEN DISMISSED? NO, RATHER I ABJURE ALL ROOFS, AND CHOOSE TO WAGE AGAINST THE ENMITY O'TH'AIR;

TO BE A COMRADE WITH THE WOLF AND OWL, NECESSITY'S SHARP PINCH!

RETURN WITH HER? WHY, THE HOT-BLOODED FRANCE, THAT DOWERLESS TOOK OUR YOUNGEST BORN — I COULD AS WELL BE BROUGHT TO KNEE HIS THRONE AND, SQUIRE-LIKE, PENSION BEG TO KEEP BASE LIFE AFOOT.

RETURN WITH HER?

PERSUADE ME RATHER TO BE SLAVE AND SUMPTER TO THIS DETESTED GROOM!

AT YOUR CHOICE, SIR.

I PRITHEE, DAUGHTER, DO NOT MAKE ME MAD: I WILL NOT TROUBLE THEE, MY CHILD; FAREWELL, WE'LL NO MORE MEET, NO MORE SEE ONE ANOTHER;

BUT YET, THOU ART MY FLESH, MY BLOOD, MY DAUGHTER.

OR RATHER A DISEASE THAT'S IN MY FLESH, WHICH I MUST NEEDS CALL MINE: THOU ART A BOIL, A PLAGUE-SORE, OR EMBOSSÈD CARBUNCLE, IN MY CORRUPTED BLOOD!

BUT I'LL NOT CHIDE THEE; LET SHAME COME WHEN IT WILL, I DO NOT CALL IT; I DO NOT BID THE THUNDER-BEARER SHOOT, NOR TELL TALES OF THEE TO HIGH-JUDGING JOVE.

MEND WHEN THOU CANST; BE BETTER AT THY LEISURE; I CAN BE PATIENT; I CAN STAY WITH REGAN, I AND MY HUNDRED KNIGHTS.

NOT ALTOGETHER SO; I LOOKED NOT FOR YOU YET, NOR AM PROVIDED FOR YOUR FIT WELCOME. GIVE EAR, SIR, TO MY SISTER; FOR THOSE THAT MINGLE REASON WITH YOUR PASSION MUST BE CONTENT TO THINK YOU OLD, AND SO ——

BUT SHE KNOWS WHAT SHE DOES.

IS THIS WELL SPOKEN?

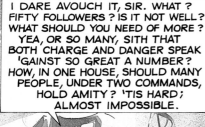

I DARE AVOUCH IT, SIR. WHAT? FIFTY FOLLOWERS? IS IT NOT WELL? WHAT SHOULD YOU NEED OF MORE? YEA, OR SO MANY, SITH THAT BOTH CHARGE AND DANGER SPEAK 'GAINST SO GREAT A NUMBER? HOW, IN ONE HOUSE, SHOULD MANY PEOPLE, UNDER TWO COMMANDS, HOLD AMITY? 'TIS HARD; ALMOST IMPOSSIBLE.

WHY MIGHT NOT YOU, MY LORD, RECEIVE ATTENDANCE FROM THOSE THAT SHE CALLS SERVANTS, OR FROM MINE?

O, REASON NOT THE NEED! OUR BASEST BEGGARS ARE IN THE POOREST THINGS SUPERFLUOUS: ALLOW NOT NATURE MORE THAN NATURE NEEDS, MAN'S LIFE IS CHEAP AS BEAST'S.

THOU ART A LADY; IF ONLY TO GO WARM WERE GORGEOUS, WHY, NATURE NEEDS NOT WHAT THOU GORGEOUS WEAR'ST, WHICH SCARCELY KEEPS THEE WARM.

BUT, FOR TRUE NEED — YOU HEAVENS, GIVE ME THAT PATIENCE, PATIENCE I NEED!

YOU SEE ME HERE, YOU GODS, A POOR OLD MAN, AS FULL OF GRIEF AS AGE; WRETCHED IN BOTH!

IF IT BE YOU THAT STIRS THESE DAUGHTERS' HEARTS AGAINST THEIR FATHER, FOOL ME NOT SO MUCH TO BEAR IT TAMELY.

TOUCH ME WITH NOBLE ANGER, AND LET NOT WOMEN'S WEAPONS — WATER-DROPS — STAIN MY MAN'S CHEEKS.

NO, YOU UNNATURAL HAGS, I WILL HAVE SUCH REVENGES ON YOU BOTH THAT ALL THE WORLD SHALL—

I WILL DO SUCH THINGS... WHAT THEY ARE, YET I KNOW NOT...

BUT THEY SHALL BE THE TERRORS OF THE EARTH!

YOU THINK I'LL WEEP? NO, I'LL NOT WEEP!

I HAVE FULL CAUSE OF WEEPING,

BUT THIS HEART SHALL BREAK INTO A HUNDRED THOUSAND FLAWS OR ERE I'LL WEEP!

O FOOL! I SHALL GO MAD!

WHO'S THERE, BESIDES FOUL WEATHER?

ENTER GENTLEMAN

ONE MINDED LIKE THE WEATHER: MOST UNQUIETLY.

I KNOW YOU. WHERE'S THE KING?

CONTENDING WITH THE FRETFUL ELEMENTS; BIDS THE WIND BLOW THE EARTH INTO THE SEA, OR SWELL THE CURLÈD WATERS 'BOVE THE MAIN, THAT THINGS MIGHT CHANGE OR CEASE; TEARS HIS WHITE HAIR WHICH THE IMPETUOUS BLASTS, WITH EYELESS RAGE, CATCH IN THEIR FURY, AND MAKE NOTHING OF;

STRIVES IN HIS LITTLE WORLD OF MAN TO OUTSTORM THE TO-AND-FRO-CONFLICTING WIND AND RAIN. THIS NIGHT, WHEREIN THE CUB-DRAWN BEAR WOULD COUCH, THE LION AND THE BELLY-PINCHÈD WOLF KEEP THEIR FUR DRY, UNBONNETED HE RUNS, AND BIDS WHAT WILL, TAKE ALL.

BUT WHO IS WITH HIM?

NONE BUT THE FOOL, WHO LABOURS TO OUT-JEST HIS HEART-STROOK INJURIES.

SIR, I DO KNOW YOU; AND DARE, UPON THE WARRANT OF MY NOTE, COMMEND A DEAR THING TO YOU.

THERE IS DIVISION (ALTHOUGH AS YET THE FACE OF IT IS COVERED WITH MUTUAL CUNNING) 'TWIXT ALBANY AND CORNWALL; WHO HAVE (AS WHO HAVE NOT, THAT THEIR GREAT STARS THRONED AND SET HIGH?) SERVANTS —WHO SEEM NO LESS— WHICH ARE TO FRANCE THE SPIES AND SPECULATIONS INTELLIGENT OF OUR STATE.

WHAT HATH BEEN SEEN, EITHER IN SNUFFS AND PACKINGS OF THE DUKES, OR THE HARD REIN WHICH BOTH OF THEM HAVE BORNE AGAINST THE OLD KIND KING; OR SOMETHING DEEPER, WHEREOF PERCHANCE THESE ARE BUT FURNISHINGS . . .

BUT, TRUE IT IS, FROM FRANCE THERE COMES A POWER INTO THIS SCATTERED KINGDOM; WHO ALREADY, WISE IN OUR NEGLIGENCE, HAVE SECRET FEET IN SOME OF OUR BEST PORTS, AND ARE AT POINT TO SHOW THEIR OPEN BANNER. NOW TO YOU:

IF ON MY CREDIT YOU DARE BUILD SO FAR TO MAKE YOUR SPEED TO DOVER, YOU SHALL FIND SOME THAT WILL THANK YOU, MAKING JUST REPORT OF HOW UNNATURAL AND BEMADDING SORROW THE KING HATH CAUSE TO PLAIN.

I AM A GENTLEMAN OF BLOOD AND BREEDING, AND FROM SOME KNOWLEDGE AND ASSURANCE OFFER THIS OFFICE TO YOU.

I WILL TALK FURTHER WITH YOU.

NO, DO NOT.

FOR CONFIRMATION THAT I AM MUCH MORE THAN MY OUT-WALL, OPEN THIS PURSE, AND TAKE WHAT IT CONTAINS.

IF YOU SHALL SEE CORDELIA —AS FEAR NOT BUT YOU SHALL— SHOW HER THIS RING, AND SHE WILL TELL YOU WHO THAT FELLOW IS THAT YET YOU DO NOT KNOW.

FIE ON THIS STORM! I WILL GO SEEK THE KING.

GIVE ME YOUR HAND. HAVE YOU NO MORE TO SAY?

FEW WORDS, BUT, TO EFFECT, MORE THAN ALL YET.

THAT, WHEN WE HAVE FOUND THE KING (IN WHICH YOUR PAIN THAT WAY, I'LL THIS) HE THAT FIRST LIGHTS ON HIM HOLLA THE OTHER.

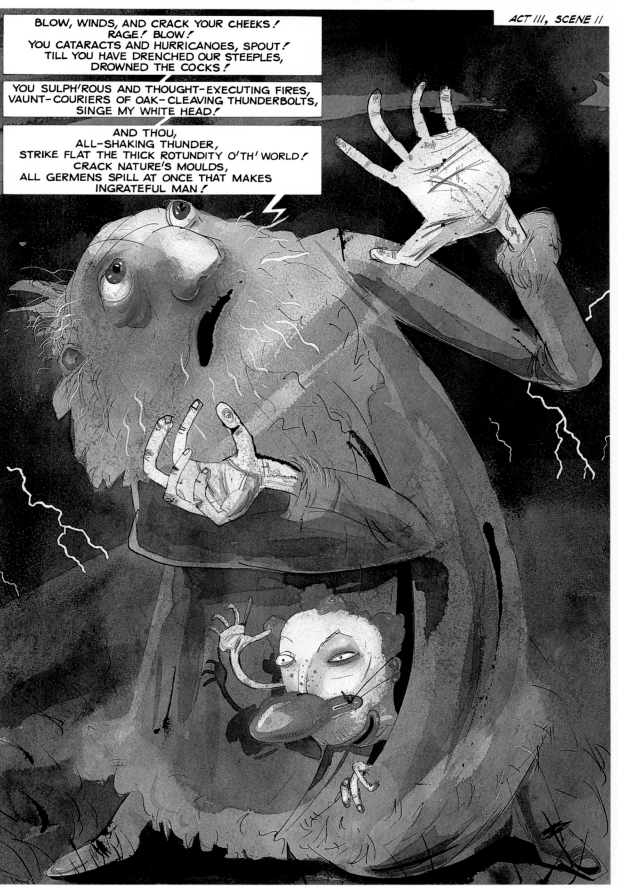

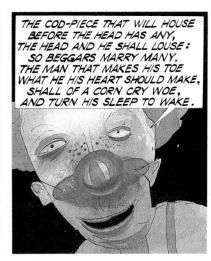

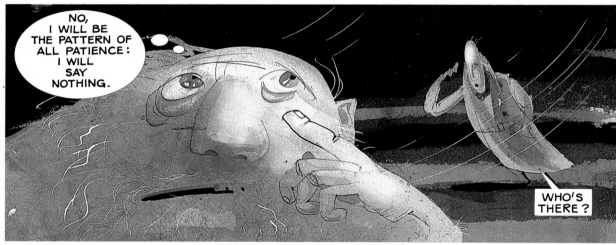

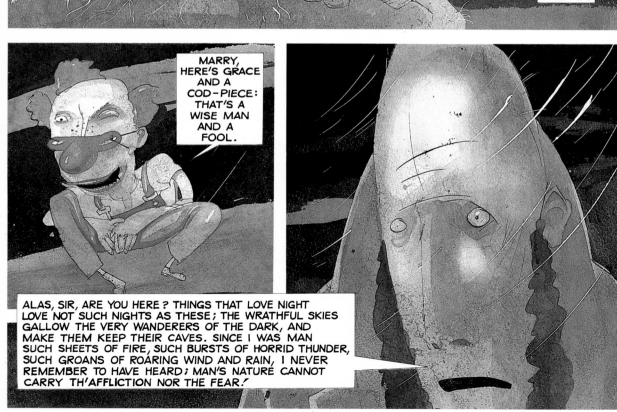

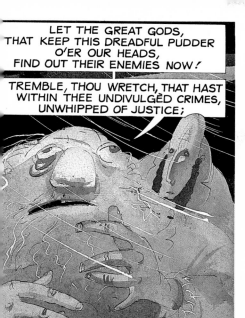
LET THE GREAT GODS, THAT KEEP THIS DREADFUL PUDDER O'ER OUR HEADS, FIND OUT THEIR ENEMIES NOW!

TREMBLE, THOU WRETCH, THAT HAST WITHIN THEE UNDIVULGÈD CRIMES, UNWHIPPED OF JUSTICE;

HIDE THEE, THOU BLOODY HAND, THOU PERJURED, AND THOU SIMULAR OF VIRTUE THAT ART INCESTUOUS;

CAITIFF, TO PIECES SHAKE, THAT UNDER COVERT AND CONVENIENT SEEMING HAS PRACTISED ON MAN'S LIFE; CLOSE PENT-UP GUILTS RIVE YOUR CONCEALING CONTINENTS, AND CRY THESE DREADFUL SUMMONERS GRACE!

I AM A MAN MORE SINNED AGAINST THAN SINNING.

ALACK! BARE-HEADED!

GRACIOUS MY LORD, HARD BY HERE IS A HOVEL; SOME FRIENDSHIP WILL IT LEND YOU 'GAINST THE TEMPEST; REPOSE YOU THERE,

WHILE I, TO THIS HARD HOUSE — (MORE HARDER THAN THE STONES WHEREOF 'TIS RAISED) WHICH EVEN BUT NOW, DEMANDING AFTER YOU, DENIED ME TO COME IN, — RETURN AND FORCE THEIR SCANTED COURTESY.

MY WITS BEGIN TO TURN.

COME ON, MY BOY.

HOW DOST, MY BOY?

ART COLD?

I AM COLD MYSELF.

WHERE IS THIS STRAW, MY FELLOW?

THE ART OF OUR NECESSITIES IS STRANGE, AND CAN MAKE VILE THINGS PRECIOUS: COME, YOUR HOVEL.

POOR FOOL AND KNAVE, I HAVE ONE PART IN MY HEART THAT'S SORRY YET FOR THEE.

72

ALACK, ALACK! EDMUND, I LIKE NOT THIS UNNATURAL DEALING.

WHEN I DESIRED THEIR LEAVE THAT I MIGHT PITY HIM, THEY TOOK FROM ME THE USE OF MINE OWN HOUSE; CHARGED ME, ON PAIN OF PERPETUAL DISPLEASURE, NEITHER TO SPEAK OF HIM, ENTREAT FOR HIM, OR ANY WAY SUSTAIN HIM.

MOST SAVAGE AND UNNATURAL!

GO TO, SAY YOU NOTHING. THERE IS DIVISION BETWEEN THE DUKES ... AND A WORSE MATTER THAN THAT.

I HAVE RECEIVED A LETTER THIS NIGHT; 'TIS DANGEROUS TO BE SPOKEN; I HAVE LOCKED THE LETTER IN MY CLOSET.

THESE INJURIES THE KING NOW BEARS WILL BE REVENGÈD HOME; THERE IS PART OF A POWER ALREADY FOOTED; WE MUST INCLINE TO THE KING.

I WILL LOOK HIM AND PRIVILY RELIEVE HIM; GO YOU AND MAINTAIN TALK WITH THE DUKE, THAT MY CHARITY BE NOT OF HIM PERCEIVED. IF HE ASK FOR ME, I AM ILL, AND GONE TO BED. IF I DIE FOR IT, AS NO LESS IS THREATENED ME, THE KING, MY OLD MASTER, MUST BE RELIEVED.

THERE IS STRANGE THINGS TOWARD, EDMUND.

PRAY YOU, BE CAREFUL.

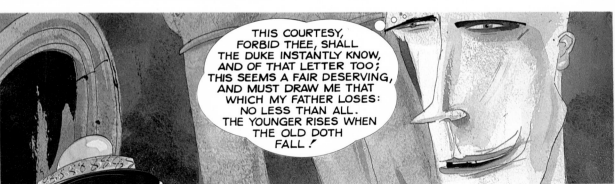

THIS COURTESY, FORBID THEE, SHALL THE DUKE INSTANTLY KNOW, AND OF THAT LETTER TOO; THIS SEEMS A FAIR DESERVING, AND MUST DRAW ME THAT WHICH MY FATHER LOSES: NO LESS THAN ALL. THE YOUNGER RISES WHEN THE OLD DOTH FALL!

ACT III, SCENE IV

HERE IS THE PLACE, MY LORD.
GOOD MY LORD, ENTER.
THE TYRANNY OF THE OPEN NIGHT'S
TOO ROUGH FOR NATURE TO ENDURE.

LET ME ALONE.

GOOD MY LORD,
ENTER HERE.

WILT BREAK
MY HEART?

I HAD RATHER
BREAK MINE OWN.

GOOD MY LORD,
ENTER.

THOU THINK'ST 'TIS MUCH
THAT THIS CONTENTIOUS STORM
INVADES US TO THE SKIN:
SO 'TIS, TO THEE; BUT WHERE
THE GREATER MALADY IS FIXED,
THE LESSER IS SCARCE FELT.

THOU'LDST SHUN A BEAR,
BUT IF THY FLIGHT LAY
TOWARD THE ROARING SEA,
THOU'LDST MEET THE BEAR
I'TH'MOUTH.

WHEN THE MIND'S FREE,
THE BODY'S DELICATE;
THE TEMPEST IN MY MIND
DOTH FROM MY SENSES
TAKE ALL FEELING ELSE
SAVE WHAT BEATS THERE
—FILIAL INGRATITUDE!

IS IT NOT AS THIS MOUTH
SHOULD TEAR THIS HAND
FOR LIFTING FOOD TO'T?

BUT I WILL PUNISH HOME:
NO, I WILL WEEP NO MORE.
IN SUCH A NIGHT
TO SHUT ME OUT?
POUR ON: I WILL ENDURE.
IN SUCH A NIGHT AS THIS?

O REGAN, GONERIL!
YOUR OLD KIND FATHER,
WHOSE FRANK HEART GAVE ALL?
O! THAT WAY MADNESS LIES!
LET ME SHUN THAT!
NO MORE OF THAT!

GOOD MY LORD, ENTER HERE.

PRITHEE GO IN THYSELF; SEEK THINE OWN EASE;

THIS TEMPEST WILL NOT GIVE ME LEAVE TO PONDER ON THINGS WOULD HURT ME MORE. BUT I'LL GO IN.

IN, BOY: GO FIRST. YOU HOUSELESS POVERTY—

NAY, GET THEE IN!

I'LL PRAY, AND THEN I'LL SLEEP.

POOR NAKED WRETCHES, WHERESO'ER YOU ARE, THAT BIDE THE PELTING OF THIS PITILESS STORM, HOW SHALL YOUR HOUSELESS HEADS AND UNFED SIDES, YOUR LOOPED AND WINDOWED RAGGEDNESS, DEFEND YOU FROM SEASONS SUCH AS THESE?

O! I HAVE TA'EN TOO LITTLE CARE OF THIS!

TAKE PHYSIC, POMP! EXPOSE THYSELF TO FEEL WHAT WRETCHES FEEL, THAT THOU MAYST SHAKE THE SUPERFLUX TO THEM, AND SHOW THE HEAVENS MORE JUST.

FATHOM AND HALF! FATHOM AND HALF!

POOR TOM!

COME NOT IN HERE, NUNCLE; HERE'S A SPIRIT!

HELP ME!

HELP ME!

GIVE ME THY HAND.

WHO'S THERE?

A SPIRIT, A SPIRIT!

HE SAYS HIS NAME'S POOR TOM.

WHAT ART THOU THAT DOST GRUMBLE THERE I'TH'STRAW? COME FORTH!

AWAY! THE FOUL FIEND FOLLOWS ME! THROUGH THE SHARP HAWTHORN BLOWS THE COLD WINDS. HUMPH! GO TO THY BED AND WARM THEE!

DIDST THOU GIVE ALL TO THY DAUGHTERS? AND ART THOU COME TO THIS?

WHO GIVES ANY THING TO POOR TOM?

WHOM THE FOUL FIEND HATH LED THROUGH FIRE AND THROUGH FLAME, THROUGH FORD AND WHIRLPOOL, O'ER BOG AND QUAGMIRE;

THAT HATH LAID KNIVES UNDER HIS PILLOW, AND HALTERS IN HIS PEW; SET RATSBANE BY HIS PORRIDGE;

MADE HIM PROUD OF HEART TO RIDE ON A BAY TROTTING-HORSE

OVER FOUR-INCHED BRIDGES; TO COURSE HIS OWN SHADOW FOR A TRAITOR.

BLESS THY FIVE WITS!

TOM'S A-COLD!

O DO-DE, DO-DE, DO-DE!

BLESS THEE FROM WHIRLWINDS, STAR-BLASTING AND TAKING.

DO POOR TOM SOME CHARITY, WHOM THE FOUL

FIEND VEXES!

THERE COULD I HAVE HIM NOW!

AND THERE!

AND THERE AGAIN!

AND THERE!

WHAT, HA'S DAUGHTERS BROUGHT HIM TO THIS PASS?

COULDST THOU SAVE NOTHING? WOULD'ST THOU GIVE 'EM ALL?

NAY, HE RESERVED A BLANKET, ELSE WE HAD BEEN ALL SHAMED.

NOW ALL THE PLAGUES THAT IN THE PENDULOUS AIR HANG FATED O'ER MEN'S FAULTS LIGHT ON THY DAUGHTERS!

HE HATH NO DAUGHTERS, SIR.

DEATH, TRAITOR! NOTHING COULD HAVE SUBDUED NATURE TO SUCH A LOWNESS BUT HIS UNKIND DAUGHTERS. IS IT THE FASHION THAT DISCARDED FATHERS SHOULD HAVE THUS LITTLE MERCY ON THEIR FLESH? JUDICIOUS PUNISHMENT: 'TWAS THIS FLESH BEGOT THOSE PELICAN DAUGHTERS.

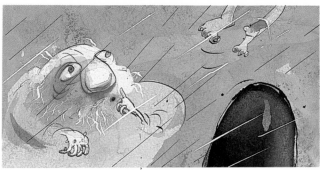

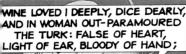

THOU WERT BETTER IN A GRAVE THAN TO ANSWER WITH THY UNCOVERED BODY THIS EXTREMITY OF THE SKIES.

IS MAN NO MORE THAN THIS? CONSIDER HIM WELL.

THOU OW'ST THE WORM NO SILK, THE BEAST NO HIDE, THE SHEEP NO WOOL, THE CAT NO PERFUME.

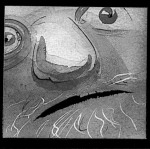

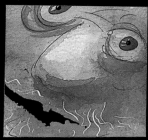

HA! HERE'S THREE ON'S ARE SOPHISTICATED; THOU ART THE THING ITSELF! UNACCOMMODATED MAN IS NO MORE BUT SUCH A POOR, BARE, FORKED ANIMAL AS THOU ART.

OFF, OFF, YOU LENDINGS!

COME, UNBUTTON HERE!

PRITHEE NUNCLE, BE CONTENTED; 'TIS A NAUGHTY NIGHT TO SWIM IN. NOW A LITTLE FIRE IN A WILD FIELD WERE LIKE AN OLD LECHER'S HEART; A SMALL SPARK, ALL THE REST ON'S BODY'S COLD.

LOOK, HERE COMES A WALKING FIRE.

THIS IS THE FOUL FLIBBERTIGIBBET: HE BEGINS AT CURFEW, AND WALKS TILL THE FIRST COCK; HE GIVES THE WEB AND THE PIN, SQUINTS THE EYE, AND MAKES THE HARE-LIP; MILDEWS THE WHITE WHEAT AND HURTS THE POOR CREATURE OF EARTH.

SWITHOLD FOOTED THRICE THE OLD; HE MET THE NIGHT-MARE AND HER NINE FOLD; BID HER ALIGHT, AND HER TROTH PLIGHT,

AND AROINT THEE, WITCH! AROINT THEE!

HOW FARES YOUR GRACE?

WHAT'S HE?

WHO'S THERE? WHAT IS'T YOU SEEK?

WHAT ARE YOU THERE?

YOUR NAMES?

POOR TOM!

THAT EATS THE SWIMMING FROG, THE TOAD, THE TADPOLE, THE WALL-NEWT AND THE WATER;

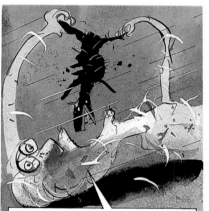

THAT IN THE FURY OF HIS HEART, WHEN THE FOUL FIEND RAGES, EATS COW-DUNG FOR SALLETS, SWALLOWS THE OLD RAT AND THE DITCH-DOG, DRINKS THE GREEN MANTLE OF THE STANDING POOL;

WHO IS WHIPPED FROM TITHING TO TITHING, AND STOCK-PUNISHED, AND IMPRISONED; WHO HATH HAD THREE SUITS TO HIS BACK, SIX SHIRTS TO HIS BODY,

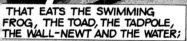

HORSE TO RIDE AND WEAPONS TO WEAR; BUT MICE AND RATS AND SUCH SMALL DEER HAVE BEEN TOM'S FOOD FOR SEVEN LONG YEAR.

BEWARE MY FOLLOWER!

PEACE, SMULKIN! PEACE, THOU FIEND!

I WILL HAVE MY REVENGE ERE I DEPART HIS HOUSE!

I NOW PERCEIVE IT WAS NOT ALTOGETHER YOUR BROTHER'S EVIL DISPOSITION MADE HIM SEEK HIS DEATH: BUT A PROVOKING MERIT, SET A-WORK BY A REPROVEABLE BADNESS IN HIMSELF.

HOW, MY LORD, I MAY BE CENSURED, THAT NATURE THUS GIVES WAY TO LOYALTY, SOMETHING FEARS ME TO THINK OF.

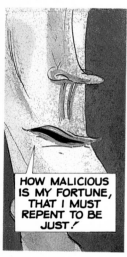

THIS IS THE LETTER HE SPOKE OF, WHICH APPROVES HIM AN INTELLIGENT PARTY TO THE ADVANTAGES OF FRANCE.

HOW MALICIOUS IS MY FORTUNE, THAT I MUST REPENT TO BE JUST!

O HEAVENS! THAT THIS TREASON WERE NOT, OR NOT I THE DETECTOR!

GO WITH ME TO THE DUCHESS.

IF THE MATTER OF THIS PAPER BE CERTAIN, YOU HAVE MIGHTY BUSINESS IN HAND.

TRUE OR FALSE IT HATH MADE THEE EARL OF GLOUCESTER. SEEK OUT WHERE THY FATHER IS, THAT HE MAY BE READY FOR OUR APPREHENSON.

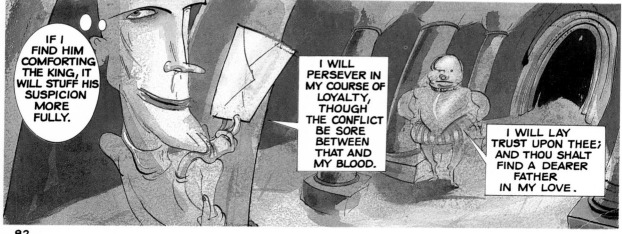

IF I FIND HIM COMFORTING THE KING, IT WILL STUFF HIS SUSPICION MORE FULLY.

I WILL PERSEVER IN MY COURSE OF LOYALTY, THOUGH THE CONFLICT BE SORE BETWEEN THAT AND MY BLOOD.

I WILL LAY TRUST UPON THEE; AND THOU SHALT FIND A DEARER FATHER IN MY LOVE.

HERE IS BETTER THAN THE OPEN AIR;
TAKE IT THANKFULLY.
I WILL PIECE OUT THE COMFORT
WITH WHAT ADDITION I CAN:
I WILL NOT BE LONG FROM YOU.

ALL THE POWER OF HIS WITS HAVE
GIVEN WAY TO HIS IMPATIENCE.
THE GODS REWARD YOUR KINDNESS.

FRATERETTO CALLS ME, AND TELLS ME NERO
IS AN ANGLER IN THE LAKE OF DARKNESS.
PRAY, INNOCENT, AND BEWARE THE FOUL FIEND!

PRITHEE, NUNCLE,
TELL ME WHETHER
A MADMAN BE
A GENTLEMAN
OR A YEOMAN.

A KING!
A KING!

NO! HE'S A YEOMAN THAT HAS
A GENTLEMAN TO HIS SON;
FOR HE'S A MAD YEOMAN
THAT SEES HIS SON
A GENTLEMAN BEFORE HIM!

TO HAVE A THOUSAND, WITH
RED BURNING SPITS, COME
HIZZING IN UPON 'EM ——

THE FOUL
FIEND BITES
MY BACK!

HE'S MAD THAT TRUSTS
IN THE TAMENESS OF
A WOLF, A HORSE'S
HEALTH, A BOY'S LOVE
OR A WHORE'S OATH!

IT SHALL BE DONE!
I WILL ARRAIGN
THEM STRAIGHT!

COME SIT
THOU HERE,
MOST
LEARNED
JUSTICER.

THOU, SAPIENT SIR,
SIT HERE.

NOW, YOU SHE-FOXES!

LOOK WHERE HE STANDS AND GLARES!

WANT'ST THOU EYES AT TRIAL, MADAM?

COME O'ER THE BOURN, BESSY, TO ME!

HER BOAT HATH A LEAK, AND SHE MUST NOT SPEAK; WHY, SHE DARES NOT COME OVER TO THEE!

THE FOUL FIEND HAUNTS POOR TOM IN THE VOICE OF A NIGHTINGALE!

HOPPEDANCE CRIES IN TOM'S BELLY FOR TWO WHITE HERRING. CROAK NOT, BLACK ANGEL: I HAVE NO FOOD FOR THEE.

HOW DO YOU, SIR? STAND YOU NOT SO AMAZED; WILL YOU LIE DOWN AND REST UPON THE CUSHIONS?

I'LL SEE THEIR TRIAL FIRST. BRING IN THEIR EVIDENCE.

THOU ROBÈD MAN OF JUSTICE, TAKE THY PLACE.

AND THOU, HIS YOKE-FELLOW OF EQUITY, BENCH BY HIS SIDE.

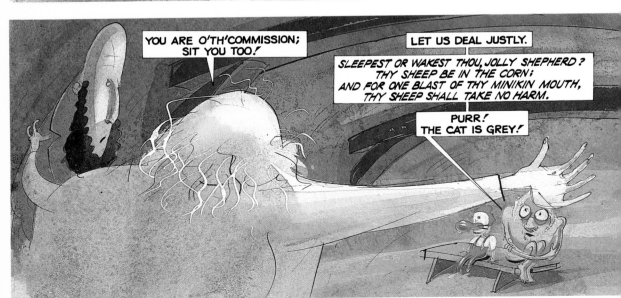

YOU ARE O'TH'COMMISSION; SIT YOU TOO!

LET US DEAL JUSTLY.

SLEEPEST OR WAKEST THOU, JOLLY SHEPHERD? THY SHEEP BE IN THE CORN; AND FOR ONE BLAST OF THY MINIKIN MOUTH, THY SHEEP SHALL TAKE NO HARM.

PURR! THE CAT IS GREY!

ARRAIGN HER FIRST: 'TIS GONERIL! I HERE TAKE MY OATH BEFORE THIS HONOURABLE ASSEMBLY, SHE KICKED THE POOR KING HER FATHER.

COME HITHER, MISTRESS. IS YOUR NAME GONERIL?

SHE CANNOT DENY IT!

CRY YOU MERCY, I TOOK YOU FOR A JOINT-STOOL!

AND HERE'S ANOTHER, WHOSE WARPED LOOKS PROCLAIM WHAT STORE HER HEART IS MADE ON.

STOP HER, THERE!

ARMS, ARMS! SWORD, FIRE! CORRUPTION IN THE PLACE! FALSE JUSTICER, WHY HAST THOU LET HER 'SCAPE?

BLESS THY FIVE WITS!

O PITY! SIR, WHERE IS THE PATIENCE NOW THAT YOU SO OFT HAVE BOASTED TO RETAIN?

MY TEARS BEGIN TO TAKE HIS PART SO MUCH, THEY MAR MY COUNTERFEITING.

THE LITTLE DOGS AND ALL — TRAY, BLANCH AND SWEETHEART — SEE, THEY BARK AT ME!

TOM WILL THROW HIS HEAD AT THEM!

AVAUNT YOU CURS!

BE THY MOUTH OR BLACK OR WHITE; TOOTH THAT POISONS IF IT BITE; MASTIFF, GREYHOUND, MONGREL GRIM, HOUND OR SPANIEL, BRACH OR LYM; OR BOBTAIL TIKE OR TRUNDLE-TAIL; TOM WILL MAKE HIM WEEP AND WAIL: FOR, WITH THROWING THUS MY HEAD,

DOGS LEAPED THE HATCH, AND ALL ARE FLED!

DO-DE, DE, DE! SESSA! COME, MARCH TO WAKES AND FAIRS AND MARKET-TOWNS. POOR TOM, THY HORN IS DRY.

THEN LET THEM ANATOMIZE REGAN: SEE WHAT BREEDS ABOUT HER HEART! IS THERE ANY CAUSE IN NATURE THAT MAKES THESE HARD HEARTS?

YOU, SIR, I ENTERTAIN FOR ONE OF MY HUNDRED; ONLY I DO NOT LIKE THE FASHION OF YOUR GARMENTS: YOU WILL SAY THEY ARE PERSIAN, BUT LET THEM BE CHANGED.

NOW, GOOD MY LORD, LIE HERE AND REST AWHILE.

MAKE NO NOISE, MAKE NO NOISE! DRAW THE CURTAINS: SO, SO.

WE'LL GO TO SUPPER I'TH' MORNING.

AND I'LL GO TO BED AT NOON.

COME HITHER, FRIEND; WHERE IS THE KING MY MASTER?

HERE, SIR; BUT TROUBLE HIM NOT, HIS WITS ARE GONE.

GOOD FRIEND, I PRITHEE TAKE HIM IN THY ARMS; I HAVE O'ERHEARD A PLOT OF DEATH UPON HIM. THERE IS A LITTER READY; LAY HIM IN'T, AND DRIVE TOWARD DOVER, FRIEND, WHERE THOU SHALT MEET BOTH WELCOME AND PROTECTION.

TAKE UP THY MASTER: IF THOU SHOULD'ST DALLY HALF AN HOUR, HIS LIFE, WITH THINE, AND ALL THAT OFFER TO DEFEND HIM, STAND IN ASSURÈD LOSS.

TAKE UP, TAKE UP; AND FOLLOW ME, THAT WILL TO SOME PROVISION GIVE THEE QUICK CONDUCT.

OPPRESSÈD NATURE SLEEPS. THIS REST MIGHT YET HAVE BALMED THY BROKEN SINEWS, WHICH, IF CONVENIENCE WILL NOT ALLOW, STAND IN HARD CURE.

COME, HELP TO BEAR THY MASTER.

THOU MUST NOT STAY BEHIND.

COME, COME AWAY.

WHEN WE OUR BETTERS SEE BEARING OUR WOES, WE SCARCELY THINK OUR MISERIES OUR FOES. WHO ALONE SUFFERS, SUFFERS MOST I'TH'MIND, LEAVING FREE THINGS AND HAPPY SHOWS BEHIND.

BUT THEN THE MIND MUCH SUFFERANCE DOTH O'ERSKIP, WHEN GRIEF HATH MATES, AND BEARING FELLOWSHIP. HOW LIGHT AND PORTABLE MY PAIN SEEMS NOW, WHEN THAT WHICH MAKES ME BEND MAKES THE KING BOW.

HE CHILDED AS I FATHERED. TOM, AWAY! MARK THE HIGH NOISES, AND THYSELF BEWRAY WHEN FALSE OPINION, WHOSE WRONG THOUGHTS DEFILE THEE, IN THY JUST PROOF REPEALS AND RECONCILES THEE.

WHAT WILL HAP MORE TONIGHT, SAFE 'SCAPE THE KING!

LURK, LURK.

ACT III, SCENE VII: GLOUCESTER'S CASTLE

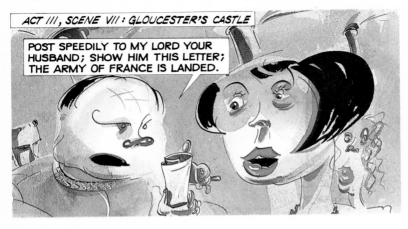

POST SPEEDILY TO MY LORD YOUR HUSBAND; SHOW HIM THIS LETTER; THE ARMY OF FRANCE IS LANDED.

SEEK OUT THE TRAITOR GLOUCESTER.

HANG HIM INSTANTLY.

PLUCK OUT HIS EYES.

LEAVE HIM TO MY DISPLEASURE.

EDMUND, KEEP YOU OUR SISTER COMPANY: THE REVENGES WE ARE BOUND TO TAKE UPON YOUR TRAITOROUS FATHER ARE NOT FIT FOR YOUR BEHOLDING.

ADVISE THE DUKE, WHERE YOU ARE GOING, TO A MOST FESTINATE PREPARATION: WE ARE BOUND TO THE LIKE. OUR POSTS SHALL BE SWIFT AND INTELLIGENT BETWIXT US.

FAREWELL, DEAR SISTER.

FAREWELL, MY LORD OF GLOUCESTER.

HOW NOW! WHERE'S THE KING?

MY LORD OF GLOUCESTER HATH CONVEYED HIM HENCE; SOME FIVE OR SIX AND THIRTY OF HIS KNIGHTS, HOT QUESTRISTS AFTER HIM, MET HIM AT GATE; WHO, WITH SOME OTHER OF THE LORD'S DEPENDANTS, ARE GONE WITH HIM TOWARD DOVER, WHERE THEY BOAST TO HAVE WELL-ARMÈD FRIENDS.

GET HORSES FOR YOUR MISTRESS.

FAREWELL, SWEET LORD, AND SISTER.

EDMUND, FAREWELL.

GO SEEK THE TRAITOR GLOUCESTER!

PINION HIM LIKE A THIEF AND BRING HIM BEFORE US.

THOUGH WELL WE MAY NOT PASS UPON HIS LIFE WITHOUT THE FORM OF JUSTICE, YET OUR POWER SHALL DO A COURT'SY TO OUR WRATH, WHICH MEN MAY BLAME BUT NOT CONTROL.

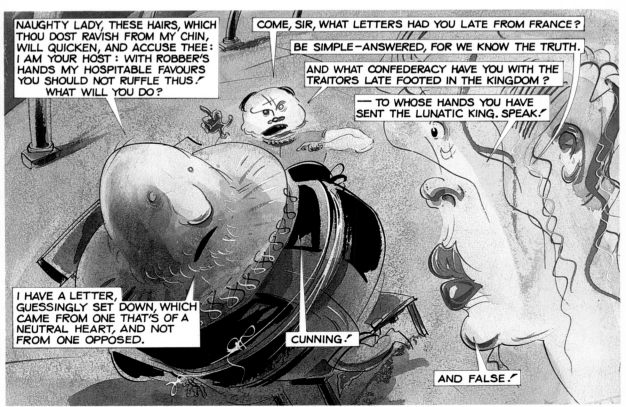

WHERE HAST THOU SENT THE KING?

TO DOVER.

WHEREFORE TO DOVER? WAST THOU NOT CHARGED AT PERIL —

WHEREFORE TO DOVER? LET HIM ANSWER THAT.!

I AM TIED TO TH'STAKE, AND I MUST STAND THE COURSE.

WHEREFORE TO DOVER?

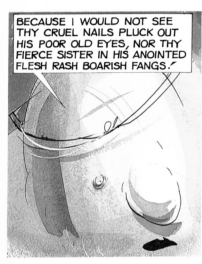

BECAUSE I WOULD NOT SEE THY CRUEL NAILS PLUCK OUT HIS POOR OLD EYES, NOR THY FIERCE SISTER IN HIS ANOINTED FLESH RASH BOARISH FANGS.!

THE SEA, WITH SUCH A STORM AS HIS BARE HEAD IN HELL-BLACK NIGHT ENDURED,

WOULD HAVE BUOYED UP, AND QUENCHED THE STELLED FIRES; YET, POOR OLD HEART, HE HOLP THE HEAVENS TO RAIN.

IF WOLVES HAD AT THY GATE HOWLED, THAT STERN TIME, THOU SHOULD'ST HAVE SAID "GOOD PORTER, TURN THE KEY."

ALL CRUELS ELSE SUBSCRIBE: BUT I SHALL SEE THE WINGÈD VENGEANCE OVERTAKE SUCH CHILDREN.!

SEE'T SHALT THOU NEVER.!

FELLOWS, HOLD THE CHAIR.!

UPON THESE EYES OF THINE I'LL SET MY FOOT.

HE THAT WILL THINK TO LIVE TILL HE BE OLD, GIVE ME SOME HELP.!

O CRUEL.!

O YOU GODS.!

ONE SIDE WILL MOCK ANOTHER.! TH'OTHER TOO.!

IF YOU SEE VENGENCE —

HOLD YOUR HAND, MY LORD; I HAVE SERVED YOU EVER SINCE I WAS A CHILD, BUT BETTER SERVICE HAVE I NEVER DONE YOU THAN NOW TO BID YOU HOLD.

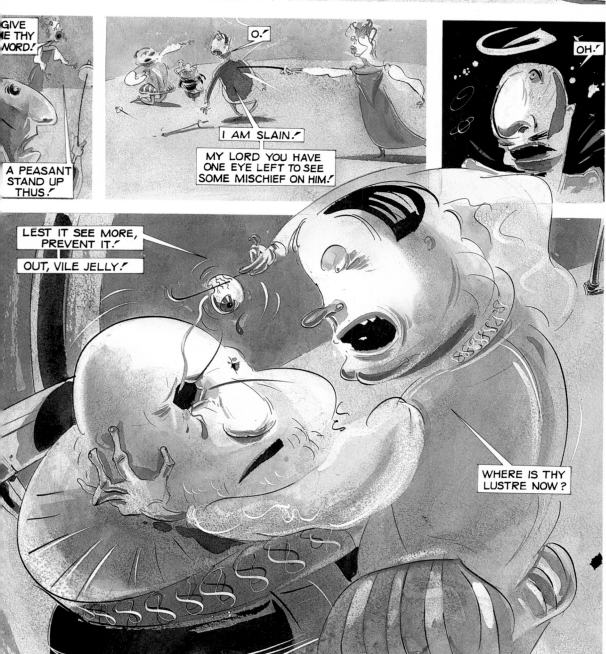

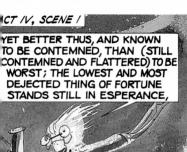

YET BETTER THUS, AND KNOWN TO BE CONTEMNED, THAN (STILL CONTEMNED AND FLATTERED) TO BE WORST; THE LOWEST AND MOST DEJECTED THING OF FORTUNE STANDS STILL IN ESPERANCE,

IVES NOT IN FEAR; THE LAMENTABLE CHANGE IS FROM THE BEST, THE WORST RETURNS TO LAUGHTER.

WELCOME, THEN, THOU UNSUBSTANTIAL AIR THAT I EMBRACE: THE WRETCH THAT THOU HAST BLOWN UNTO THE WORST OWES NOTHING TO THY BLASTS.

BUT WHO COMES HERE?

MY FATHER, POORLY LED?

WORLD, WORLD, O WORLD!

BUT THAT THY STRANGE MUTATIONS MAKE US HATE THEE, LIFE WOULD NOT YIELD TO AGE.

O, MY GOOD LORD, I HAVE BEEN YOUR TENANT, AND YOUR FATHER'S TENANT, THESE FOURSCORE YEARS.

AWAY! GET THEE AWAY! GOOD FRIEND, BE GONE: THY COMFORTS CAN DO ME NO GOOD AT ALL; THEE THEY MAY HURT.

YOU CANNOT SEE YOUR WAY!

I HAVE NO WAY, AND THEREFORE WANT NO EYES: I STUMBLED WHEN I SAW.

FULL OFT 'TIS SEEN, OUR MEANS SECURE US, AND OUR MERE DEFECTS PROVE OUR COMMODITIES.

OH! DEAR SON EDGAR, THE FOOD, OF THY ABUSĔD FATHER'S WRATH,

MIGHT I BUT LIVE TO SEE THEE IN MY TOUCH, I'D SAY I HAD EYES AGAIN!

HOW NOW! WHO'S THERE?

'TIS POOR MAD TOM!

O GODS! WHO IS'T CAN SAY "I AM AT THE WORST"?

I AM WORSE THAN E'ER I WAS.

AND WORSE I MAY BE YET. THE WORST IS NOT, SO LONG AS WE CAN SAY "THIS IS THE WORST".

FELLOW, WHERE GOEST?

IS IT A BEGGAR-MAN?

MADMAN AND BEGGAR TOO!

HE HAS SOME REASON, ELSE HE COULD NOT BEG. I'TH'LAST NIGHT'S STORM, I SUCH A FELLOW SAW, WHICH MADE ME THINK A MAN A WORM.

MY SON CAME THEN INTO MY MIND; AND YET MY MIND WAS THEN SCARCE FRIENDS WITH HIM. I HAVE HEARD MORE SINCE; AS FLIES TO WANTON BOYS ARE WE TO TH'GODS: THEY KILL US FOR THEIR SPORT.

HOW SHOULD THIS BE?

BAD IS THE TRADE THAT MUST PLAY FOOL TO SORROW, ANG'RING ITSELF AND OTHERS.

BLESS THEE, MASTER!

IS THAT THE NAKED FELLOW?

AY, MY LORD.

THEN, PRITHEE, GET THEE AWAY. IF, FOR MY SAKE, THOU WILT O'ERTAKE US HENCE A MILE OR TWAIN, I'TH'WAY TOWARD DOVER, DO IT FOR ANCIENT LOVE, AND BRING SOME COVERING FOR THIS NAKED SOUL, WHICH I'LL ENTREAT TO LEAD ME.

ALACK, SIR, HE IS MAD!

'TIS THE TIMES' PLAGUE, WHEN MADMEN LEAD THE BLIND. DO AS I BID THEE! OR RATHER, DO THY PLEASURE. ABOVE THE REST: BE GONE!

I'LL BRING HIM THE BEST 'PAREL THAT I HAVE. COME ON'T WHAT WILL.

SIRRAH? NAKED FELLOW?

POOR TOM'S A-COLD!

I CANNOT DAUB IT FURTHER!

COME HITHER, FELLOW!

AND YET, I MUST.

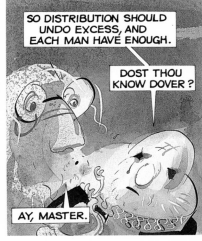

WELCOME, MY LORD. I MARVEL OUR MILD HUSBAND NOT MET US ON THE WAY!

NOW WHERE'S YOUR MASTER?

MADAM, WITHIN; BUT NEVER MAN SO CHANGED. I TOLD HIM OF THE ARMY THAT WAS LANDED:

HE SMILED AT IT!

I TOLD HIM YOU WERE COMING; HIS ANSWER WAS "THE WORSE".

OF GLOUCESTER'S TREACHERY, AND OF THE LOYAL SERVICE OF HIS SON, WHEN I INFORMED HIM, THEN HE CALLED ME "SOT", AND TOLD ME I HAD TURNED THE WRONG SIDE OUT.

WHAT MOST HE SHOULD DISLIKE SEEMS PLEASANT TO HIM; WHAT LIKE, OFFENSIVE.

THEN SHALL YOU GO NO FURTHER. IT IS THE COWISH TERROR OF HIS SPIRIT THAT DARES NOT UNDERTAKE; HE'LL NOT FEEL WRONGS WHICH TIE HIM TO AN ANSWER.

OUR WISHES ON THE WAY MAY PROVE EFFECTS.

BACK, EDMUND, TO MY BROTHER; HASTEN HIS MUSTERS AND CONDUCT HIS POWERS.

I MUST CHANGE ARMS AT HOME, AND GIVE THE DISTAFF INTO MY HUSBAND'S HANDS. THIS TRUSTY SERVANT SHALL PASS BETWEEN US.

ERE LONG YOU ARE LIKE TO HEAR — IF YOU DARE VENTURE IN YOUR OWN BEHALF — A MISTRESS'S COMMAND.

WEAR THIS.

SPARE SPEECH.

DECLINE YOUR HEAD.

THIS KISS...

IF IT DURST SPEAK, WOULD STRETCH THY SPIRITS UP INTO THE AIR.

CONCEIVE, AND FARE THEE WELL.

YOURS IN THE RANKS OF DEATH.

MY MOST DEAR GLOUCESTER.

OH! THE DIFFERENCE OF MAN AND MAN! TO THEE A WOMAN'S SERVICES ARE DUE.

A FOOL USURPS MY BED!

MADAM! HERE COMES MY LORD!

I HAVE BEEN WORTH THE WHISTLE!

O GONERIL, YOU ARE NOT WORTH THE DUST WHICH THE RUDE WIND BLOWS IN YOUR FACE!

I FEAR YOUR DISPOSITION: THAT NATURE WHICH CONTEMNS ITS ORIGIN CANNOT BE BORDERED CERTAIN IN ITSELF; SHE THAT HERSELF WILL SLIVER AND DISBRANCH FROM HER MATERIAL SAP, PERFORCE MUST WITHER, AND COME TO DEADLY USE!

NO MORE! THE TEXT IS FOOLISH!

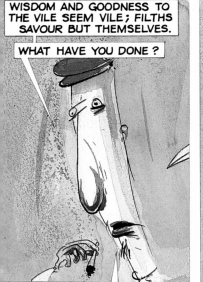

WISDOM AND GOODNESS TO THE VILE SEEM VILE; FILTHS SAVOUR BUT THEMSELVES.

WHAT HAVE YOU DONE?

TIGERS, NOT DAUGHTERS: WHAT HAVE YOU PERFORMED?

A FATHER, AND A GRACIOUS AGED MAN, WHOSE REVERENCE EVEN THE HEAD-LUGGED BEAR WOULD LICK, (MOST BARBAROUS, MOST DEGENERATE!) HAVE YOU MADDED!

COULD MY GOOD BROTHER SUFFER YOU TO DO IT?

A MAN, A PRINCE, BY HIM SO BENEFITED?

IF THAT THE HEAVENS DO NOT THEIR VISIBLE SPIRITS SEND QUICKLY DOWN TO TAME THESE WILD OFFENCES, IT WILL COME HUMANITY MUST PERFORCE PREY ON ITSELF, LIKE MONSTERS OF THE DEEP!

MILK-LIVERED MAN! THAT BEAR'ST A CHEEK FOR BLOWS, A HEAD FOR WRONGS; WHO HAST NOT IN THY BROWS AN EYE DISCERNING THINE HONOUR FROM THY SUFFERING; THAT NOT KNOW'ST FOOLS DO THOSE VILLAINS PITY WHO ARE PUNISHED ERE THEY HAVE DONE THEIR MISCHIEF!

WHERE'S THY DRUM?

FRANCE SPREADS HIS BANNERS IN OUR NOISELESS LAND, WITH PLUMÈD HELM THY STATE BEGINS TO THREAT, WHILST THOU, A MORAL FOOL, SITS STILL AND CRIES "ALACK! WHY DOES HE SO?"

SEE THYSELF, DEVIL! PROPER DEFORMITY SHOWS NOT IN THE FIEND SO HORRID AS IN WOMAN.

O VAIN FOOL!

THOU CHANGÈD AND SELF-COVERED THING, FOR SHAME! BE-MONSTER NOT THY FEATURE!

WERE'T MY FITNESS TO LET THESE HANDS OBEY MY BLOOD, THEY ARE APT ENOUGH TO DISLOCATE AND TEAR THY FLESH AND BONES!

HOWE'ER THOU ART A FIEND, A WOMAN'S SHAPE DOTH SHIELD THEE.

MARRY, YOUR MANHOOD! MEW!

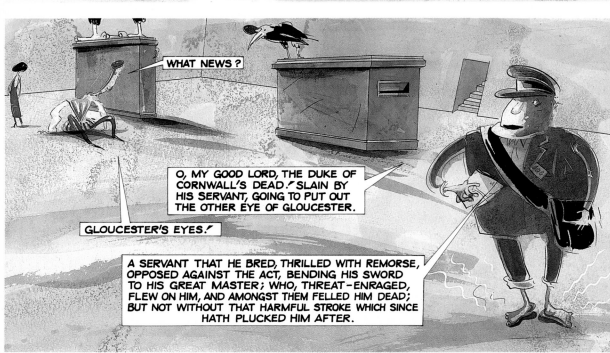

WHAT NEWS?

O, MY GOOD LORD, THE DUKE OF CORNWALL'S DEAD! SLAIN BY HIS SERVANT, GOING TO PUT OUT THE OTHER EYE OF GLOUCESTER.

GLOUCESTER'S EYES!

A SERVANT THAT HE BRED, THRILLED WITH REMORSE, OPPOSED AGAINST THE ACT, BENDING HIS SWORD TO HIS GREAT MASTER; WHO, THREAT-ENRAGED, FLEW ON HIM, AND AMONGST THEM FELLED HIM DEAD; BUT NOT WITHOUT THAT HARMFUL STROKE WHICH SINCE HATH PLUCKED HIM AFTER.

THIS SHOWS YOU ARE ABOVE, YOU JUSTICERS, THAT THESE OUR NETHER CRIMES SO SPEEDILY CAN VENGE!

BUT O, POOR GLOUCESTER! LOST HE HIS OTHER EYE?

BOTH, BOTH, MY LORD.

THIS LETTER, MADAM, CRAVES A SPEEDY ANSWER: 'TIS FROM YOUR SISTER.

ONE WAY I LIKE THIS WELL! BUT, BEING WIDOW, AND MY GLOUCESTER WITH HER, MAY ALL THE BUILDING IN MY FANCY PLUCK UPON MY HATEFUL LIFE: ANOTHER WAY, THE NEWS IS NOT SO TART.

I'LL READ, AND ANSWER.

WHERE WAS HIS SON WHEN THEY DID TAKE HIS EYES?

COME WITH MY LADY, HITHER.

HE IS NOT HERE.

NO, MY GOOD LORD; I MET HIM BACK AGAIN.

KNOWS HE THE WICKEDNESS?

AY, MY GOOD LORD.

'TWAS HE INFORMED AGAINST HIM, AND QUIT THE HOUSE ON PURPOSE THAT THEIR PUNISHMENT MIGHT HAVE THE FREER COURSE.

GLOUCESTER, I LIVE TO THANK THEE FOR THE LOVE THOU SHOW'DST THE KING, AND TO REVENGE THINE EYES.

COME HITHER, FRIEND: TELL ME WHAT MORE THOU KNOW'ST.

99

WHY THE KING OF FRANCE IS SO SUDDENLY GONE BACK, KNOW YOU NO REASON?

SOMETHING HE LEFT IMPERFECT IN THE STATE, WHICH SINCE HIS COMING FORTH IS THOUGHT OF; WHICH IMPORTS TO THE KINGDOM SO MUCH FEAR AND DANGER THAT HIS PERSONAL RETURN WAS MOST REQUIRED AND NECESSARY.

WHO HATH HE LEFT BEHIND HIM GENERAL?

THE MARSHAL OF FRANCE, MONSIEUR LA FAR.

DID YOUR LETTERS PIERCE THE QUEEN TO ANY DEMONSTRATION OF GRIEF?

AY, SIR; SHE TOOK THEM, READ THEM IN MY PRESENCE; AND NOW AND THEN AN AMPLE TEAR TRILLED DOWN HER DELICATE CHEEK; IT SEEMED SHE WAS A QUEEN OVER HER PASSION, WHO MOST REBEL-LIKE SOUGHT TO BE KING O'ER HER.

O, THEN IT MOVED HER?

NOT TO A RAGE; PATIENCE AND SORROW STROVE WHO SHOULD EXPRESS HER GOODLIEST. YOU HAVE SEEN SUNSHINE AND RAIN AT ONCE; HER SMILES AND TEARS WERE LIKE, A BETTER WAY; THOSE HAPPY SMILETS THAT PLAYED ON HER RIPE LIP SEEMED NOT TO KNOW WHAT GUESTS WERE IN HER EYES, WHICH PARTED THENCE AS PEARLS FROM DIAMONDS DROPPED.

IN BRIEF, SORROW WOULD BE A RARITY MOST BELOVED, IF ALL COULD SO BECOME IT.

MADE SHE NO VERBAL QUESTION?

FAITH, ONCE OR TWICE SHE HEAVED THE NAME OF "FATHER" PANTINGLY FORTH, AS IF IT PRESSED HER HEART; CRIED "SISTERS! SISTERS! SHAME OF LADIES! SISTERS! KENT! FATHER! SISTERS! WHAT? I'TH' STORM? I'TH' NIGHT? LET PITY NOT BELIEVE IT!"

THERE SHE SHOOK THE HOLY WATER FROM HER HEAVENLY EYES AND CLAMOUR MOISTENED, THEN AWAY SHE STARTED, TO DEAL WITH GRIEF ALONE.

IT IS THE STARS, THE STARS ABOVE US, GOVERN OUR CONDITIONS; ELSE ONE SELF MATE AND MAKE COULD NOT BEGET SUCH DIFFERENT ISSUES.

YOU SPOKE NOT WITH HER SINCE?

NO.

WAS THIS BEFORE THE KING RETURNED?

NO, SINCE.

WELL, SIR, THE POOR DISTRESSED LEAR'S I'TH'TOWN; WHO SOMETIME, IN HIS BETTER TUNE, REMEMBERS WHAT WE ARE COME ABOUT; AND BY NO MEANS WILL YIELD TO SEE HIS DAUGHTER.

WHY, GOOD SIR?

A SOVEREIGN SHAME SO ELBOWS HIM: HIS OWN UNKINDNESS, THAT STRIPPED HER FROM HIS BENEDICTION, TURNED HER TO FOREIGN CASUALTIES, GAVE HER DEAR RIGHTS TO HIS DOG-HEARTED DAUGHTERS—

THESE THINGS STING HIS MIND SO VENOMOUSLY THAT BURNING SHAME DETAINS HIM FROM CORDELIA.

ALACK! POOR GENTLEMAN.

OF ALBANY'S AND CORNWALL'S POWERS YOU HEARD NOT?

'TIS SO, THEY ARE AFOOT.

WELL, SIR, I'LL BRING YOU TO OUR MASTER LEAR, AND LEAVE YOU TO ATTEND HIM. SOME DEAR CAUSE WILL IN CONCEALMENT WRAP ME UP AWHILE; WHEN I AM KNOWN ARIGHT, YOU SHALL NOT GRIEVE LENDING ME THIS ACQUAINTANCE.

I PRAY YOU, GO ALONG WITH ME.

ALACK! 'TIS HE: WHY, HE WAS MET EVEN NOW, AS MAD AS THE VEXED SEA, SINGING ALOUD, CROWNED WITH RANK FUMITER AND FURROW-WEEDS, WITH HARDOCKS, HEMLOCK, NETTLES, CUCKOO-FLOWERS, DARNEL AND ALL THE IDLE WEEDS THAT GROW IN OUR SUSTAINING CORN.

A CENTURY SEND FORTH; SEARCH EVERY ACRE IN THE HIGH-GROWN FIELD AND BRING HIM TO OUR EYE.

WHAT CAN MAN'S WISDOM IN THE RESTORING HIS BEREAVED SENSE? HE THAT HELPS HIM, TAKE ALL MY OUTWARD WORTH.

THERE IS MEANS, MADAM. OUR FOSTER-NURSE OF NATURE IS REPOSE, THE WHICH HE LACKS; THAT TO PROVOKE IN HIM, ARE MANY SIMPLES OPERATIVE, WHOSE POWER WILL CLOSE THE EYE OF ANGUISH.

ALL BLESSED SECRETS, ALL YOU UNPUBLISHED VIRTUES OF THE EARTH, SPRING WITH MY TEARS! BE AIDANT AND REMEDIATE IN THE GOOD MAN'S DISTRESS!

SEEK, SEEK FOR HIM, LEST HIS UNGOVERNED RAGE DISSOLVE THE LIFE THAT WANTS THE MEANS TO LEAD IT!

NEWS, MADAM! THE BRITISH POWERS ARE MARCHING HITHERWARD!

'TIS KNOWN BEFORE; OUR PREPARATION STANDS IN EXPECTATION OF THEM.

O DEAR FATHER! IT IS THY BUSINESS THAT I GO ABOUT; THEREFORE GREAT FRANCE MY MOURNING AND IMPORTUNED TEARS HATH PITIED.

NO BLOWN AMBITION DOTH OUR ARMS INCITE, BUT LOVE, DEAR LOVE, AND OUR AGED FATHER'S RIGHT. SOON MAY I HEAR AND SEE HIM!

ACT IV, SCENE V
GLOUCESTER'S CASTLE

BUT ARE MY BROTHER'S POWERS SET FORTH?

AY, MADAM.

HIMSELF IN PERSON THERE?

MADAM, WITH MUCH ADO. YOUR SISTER IS THE BETTER SOLDIER.

LORD EDMUND SPAKE NOT WITH YOUR LORD AT HOME?

NO, MADAM.

WHAT MIGHT IMPORT MY SISTER'S LETTER TO HIM?

I KNOW NOT, LADY.

FAITH, HE IS POSTED HENCE, ON SERIOUS MATTER. IT WAS GREAT IGNORANCE, GLOUCESTER'S EYES BEING OUT, TO LET HIM LIVE; WHERE HE ARRIVES HE MOVES ALL HEARTS AGAINST US. EDMUND, I THINK, IS GONE, IN PITY OF HIS MISERY, TO DISPATCH HIS NIGHTED LIFE;

MOREOVER, TO DESCRY THE STRENGTH O'TH'ENEMY.

I MUST NEEDS AFTER HIM, MADAM, WITH MY LETTER.

OUR TROOPS SET FORTH TOMORROW; STAY WITH US: THE WAYS ARE DANGEROUS.

I MAY NOT, MADAM: MY LADY CHARGED MY DUTY IN THIS BUSINESS.

WHY SHOULD SHE WRITE
TO EDMUND ? MIGHT NOT YOU
TRANSPORT HER PURPOSES
BY WORD ?
BELIKE SOME THINGS —
I KNOW NOT WHAT.
I'LL LOVE THEE MUCH:
LET ME UNSEAL THE LETTER.

MADAM,
I HAD RATHER —

I KNOW YOUR LADY DOES NOT
LOVE HER HUSBAND; I AM SURE
OF THAT. AND AT HER LATE BEING
HERE, SHE GAVE STRANGE
ŒILLIADS AND MOST SPEAKING
LOOKS TO NOBLE EDMUND.

I KNOW YOU ARE OF HER BOSOM

I, MADAM

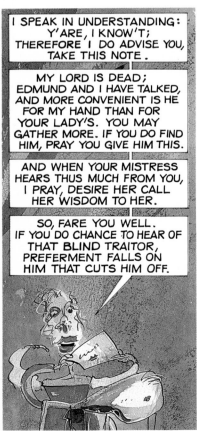

I SPEAK IN UNDERSTANDING:
Y'ARE, I KNOW'T;
THEREFORE I DO ADVISE YOU,
TAKE THIS NOTE .

MY LORD IS DEAD;
EDMUND AND I HAVE TALKED,
AND MORE CONVENIENT IS HE
FOR MY HAND THAN FOR
YOUR LADY'S. YOU MAY
GATHER MORE. IF YOU DO FIND
HIM, PRAY YOU GIVE HIM THIS.

AND WHEN YOUR MISTRESS
HEARS THUS MUCH FROM YOU,
I PRAY, DESIRE HER CALL
HER WISDOM TO HER.

SO, FARE YOU WELL.
IF YOU DO CHANCE TO HEAR OF
THAT BLIND TRAITOR,
PREFERMENT FALLS ON
HIM THAT CUTS HIM OFF.

WOULD I COULD
MEET HIM, MADAM:
I SHOULD SHOW WHAT
PARTY I DO FOLLOW.

FARE
THEE
WELL.

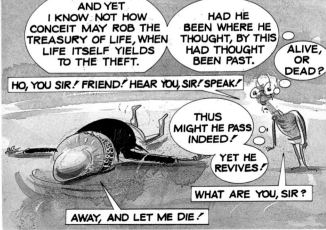

HADST THOU BEEN AUGHT BUT GOSSAMER, FEATHERS, AIR — SO MANY FATHOMS DOWN PRECIPITATING — THOU'DST SHIVERED LIKE AN EGG; BUT THOU DOST BREATHE, HAST HEAVY SUBSTANCE, BLEED'ST NOT, SPEAK'ST, ART SOUND.

TEN MASTS AT EACH MAKE NOT THE ALTITUDE WHICH THOU HADST PERPENDICULARLY FELL: THY LIFE'S A MIRACLE.

SPEAK YET AGAIN.

BUT HAVE I FALL'N OR NO?

FROM THE DREAD SUMMIT OF THIS CHALKY BOURN.

LOOK UP A-HEIGHT.

THE SHRILL-GORGED LARK SO FAR CANNOT BE SEEN OR HEARD.

DO BUT LOOK UP.

ALACK, I HAVE NO EYES!

IS WRETCHEDNESS DEPRIVED THAT BENEFIT TO END ITSELF BY DEATH?

'TWAS YET SOME COMFORT WHEN MISERY COULD BEGUILE THE TYRANT'S RAGE, AND FRUSTRATE HIS PROUD WILL.

GIVE ME YOUR ARM.

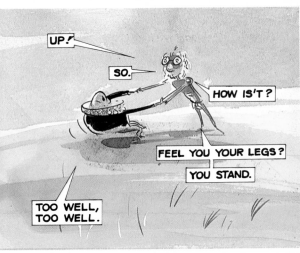

UP.

SO.

HOW IS'T?

FEEL YOU YOUR LEGS?

YOU STAND.

TOO WELL, TOO WELL.

THIS IS ABOVE ALL STRANGENESS. UPON THE CROWN O'TH'CLIFF, WHAT THING WAS THAT WHICH PARTED FROM YOU?

A POOR UNFORTUNATE BEGGAR.

AS I STOOD HERE BELOW, METHOUGHT HIS EYES WERE TWO FULL MOONS! HE HAD A THOUSAND NOSES, HORNS WHELKED AND WAVED LIKE THE ENRIDGÈD SEA!

IT WAS SOME FIEND!

THEREFORE, THOU HAPPY FATHER, THINK THAT THE CLEAREST GODS, WHO MAKE THEM HONOURS OF MEN'S IMPOSSIBILITIES, HAVE PRESERVÈD THEE.

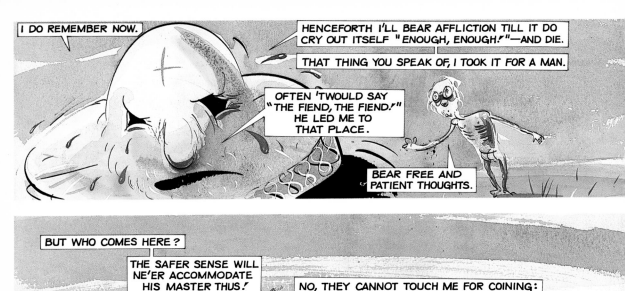

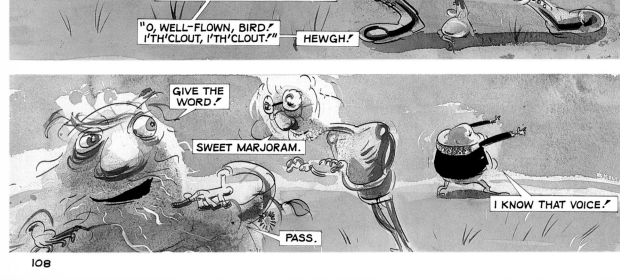

HA! GONERIL WITH A WHITE BEARD! THEY FLATTERED ME LIKE A DOG, AND TOLD ME I HAD THE WHITE HAIRS IN MY BEARD ERE THE BLACK ONES WERE THERE. TO SAY "AY" AND "NO" TO EVERYTHING THAT I SAID!

"AY" AND "NO" TOO WAS NO GOOD DIVINITY!

WHEN THE RAIN CAME TO WET ME ONCE, AND THE WIND TO MAKE ME CHATTER, WHEN THE THUNDER WOULD NOT PEACE AT MY BIDDING — THERE I FOUND 'EM, THERE I SMELT 'EM OUT!

GO TO: THEY ARE NOT MEN O'THEIR WORDS.

THEY TOLD ME I WAS EVERYTHING; 'TIS A LIE! I AM NOT AGUE - PROOF.

THE TRICK OF THAT VOICE I DO WELL REMEMBER: IS'T NOT THE KING?

AY, EVERY INCH A KING: WHEN I DO STARE, SEE HOW THE SUBJECT QUAKES! "I PARDON THAT MAN'S LIFE! WHAT WAS THY CAUSE? ADULTERY? THOU SHALT NOT DIE!" DIE FOR ADULTERY? NO: THE WREN GOES TO 'T, AND THE SMALL GUILDED FLY DOES LECHER IN MY SIGHT. LET COPULATION THRIVE!

FOR GLOUCESTER'S BASTARD SON WAS KINDER TO HIS FATHER THAN MY DAUGHTERS GOT 'TWEEN THE LAWFUL SHEETS.

TO 'T, LUXURY, PELL-MELL! FOR I LACK SOLDIERS!

BEHOLD YON SIMP'RING DAME, WHOSE FACE BETWEEN HER FORKS PRESAGES SNOW; THAT MINCES VIRTUE AND DOES SHAKE THE HEAD TO HEAR OF PLEASURE'S NAME.

THE FITCHEW NOR THE SOILED HORSE GOES TO 'T WITH A MORE RIOTOUS APPETITE!

DOWN FROM THE WAIST THEY ARE CENTAURS, THOUGH WOMEN ALL ABOVE!

BUT TO THE GIRDLE DO THE GODS INHERIT; BENEATH IS ALL THE FIEND'S!

THERE'S HELL, THERE'S DARKNESS, THERE IS THE SULPHUROUS PIT!

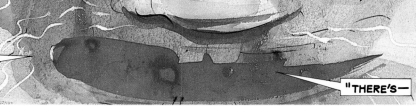

— BURNING! SCALDING! STENCH! CONSUMPTION! FIE, FIE, FIE! PAH! PAH! "GIVE ME AN OUNCE OF CIVET, GOOD APOTHECARY, TO SWEETEN MY IMAGINATION."

"THERE'S—

WHAT, ART MAD? A MAN MAY SEE HOW THIS WORLD GOES, WITH NO EYES! LOOK WITH THINE EARS: SEE HOW YOND JUSTICE RAILS UPON YOND SIMPLE THIEF.

HARK, IN THINE EAR: CHANGE PLACES, AND, HANDY-DANDY, WHICH IS THE JUSTICE, WHICH IS THE THIEF?

THOU HAST SEEN A FARMER'S DOG BARK AT A BEGGAR?

AY, SIR.

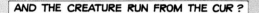

AND THE CREATURE RUN FROM THE CUR?

THERE THOU MIGHT'ST BEHOLD THE GREAT IMAGE OF AUTHORITY:

A DOG'S OBEYED IN OFFICE!

"THOU RASCAL BEADLE, HOLD THY BLOODY HAND! WHY DOST THOU LASH THAT WHORE? STRIP THINE OWN BACK! THOU HOTLY LUSTS TO USE HER IN THAT KIND FOR WHICH THOU WHIPP'ST HER!"

THE USURER HANGS THE COZENER. THOROUGH TATTERED CLOTHES GREAT VICES DO APPEAR; ROBES AND FURRED GOWNS HIDE ALL.

PLATE SIN WITH GOLD, AND THE STRONG LANCE OF JUSTICE HURTLESS BREAKS; ARM IT IN RAGS, A PYGMY'S STRAW DOES PIERCE IT.

NONE DOES OFFEND, NONE I SAY, NONE! I'LL ABLE 'EM!

TAKE THAT OF ME, MY FRIEND, WHO HAVE THE POWER TO SEAL TH'ACCUSER'S LIPS. GET THEE GLASS EYES, AND, LIKE A SCURVY POLITICIAN, SEEM TO SEE THE THINGS THOU DOST NOT.

NOW, NOW, NOW, NOW: PULL OFF MY BOOTS!

HARDER, HARDER!

SO.

O, MATTER AND IMPERTINENCY MIXED! REASON IN MADNESS!

NO SECONDS? ALL MYSELF? WHY THIS WOULD MAKE A MAN A MAN OF SALT, TO USE HIS EYES FOR GARDEN WATER-POTS, AY, AND LAYING AUTUMN'S DUST. I WILL DIE BRAVELY, LIKE A SMUG BRIDEGROOM, WHAT! I WILL BE JOVIAL! COME, COME; I AM A KING, MASTERS, KNOW YOU THAT?

YOU ARE A ROYAL ONE, AND WE OBEY YOU.

THEN THERE'S LIFE IN'T! COME: AND YOU GET IT, YOU SHALL GET IT BY RUNNING.

SA, SA, SA, SA!

A SIGHT MOST PITIFUL IN THE MEANEST WRETCH; PAST SPEAKING OF IN A KING!

THOU HAST ONE DAUGHTER WHO REDEEMS NATURE FROM THE GENERAL CURSE WHICH TWAIN HAVE BROUGHT HER TO.

HAIL, GENTLE SIR!

SIR, SPEED YOU: WHAT'S YOUR WILL?

DO YOU HEAR AUGHT, SIR, OF A BATTLE TOWARD?

MOST SURE AND VULGAR; EVERYONE HEARS THAT, WHICH CAN DISTINGUISH SOUND.

BUT, BY YOUR FAVOUR, HOW NEAR'S THE OTHER ARMY?

NEAR, AND ON SPEEDY FOOT; THE MAIN DESCRY STANDS ON THE HOURLY THOUGHT.

I THANK YOU, SIR; THAT'S ALL.

THOUGH THAT THE QUEEN ON SPECIAL CAUSE IS HERE, HER ARMY IS MOVED ON.

I THANK YOU, SIR.

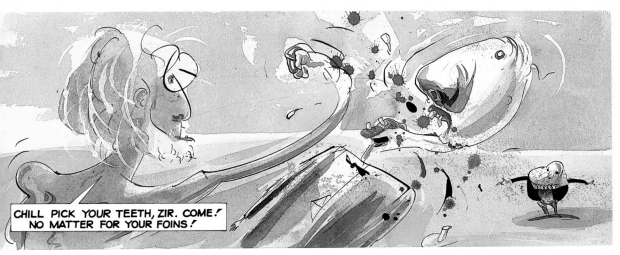

CHILL PICK YOUR TEETH, ZIR. COME! NO MATTER FOR YOUR FOINS!

SLAVE, THOU HAST SLAIN ME! VILLAIN, TAKE MY PURSE. IF EVER THOU WILT THRIVE, BURY MY BODY; AND GIVE THE LETTERS WHICH THOU FIND'ST ABOUT ME TO EDMUND EARL OF GLOUCESTER: SEEK HIM OUT UPON THE ENGLISH PARTY.

O! UNTIMELY DEATH.

DEATH!

I KNOW THEE WELL: A SERVICEABLE VILLAIN; AS DUTEOUS TO THE VICES OF THY MISTRESS AS BADNESS WOULD DESIRE.

WHAT! IS HE DEAD?

SIT YOU DOWN, FATHER; REST YOU.

LET'S SEE THESE POCKETS:

THE LETTERS THAT HE SPEAKS OF MAY BE MY FRIENDS.

HE'S DEAD.

I AM ONLY SORRY HE HAD NO OTHER DEATHSMAN.

LET US SEE: LEAVE, GENTLE WAX; AND, MANNERS, BLAME US NOT.

TO KNOW OUR ENEMIES' MINDS, WE RIP THEIR HEARTS; THEIR PAPERS IS MORE LAWFUL.

Let our reciprocal vows be remembered ~

You have many opportunities to cut him off; if your will want not, time and place will be fruitfully offered.

There is nothing done if he return the conqueror; then am I the prisoner, and his bed my gaol ~ from the loathed warmth whereof, deliver me! and supply the place for your labour ~

your ~
wife, so I would say! ~
affectionate
servant,
Goneril ~

O INDISTINGUISHED SPACE OF WOMAN'S WILL! A PLOT UPON HER VIRTUOUS HUSBAND'S LIFE!

AND THE EXCHANGE — MY BROTHER!

HERE, IN THE SANDS, THEE I'LL RAKE UP (THE POST UNSANCTIFIED OF MURDEROUS LECHERS)

AND IN THE MATURE TIME WITH THIS UNGRACIOUS PAPER STRIKE THE SIGHT OF THE DEATH-PRACTISED DUKE!

FOR HIM 'TIS WELL THAT OF THY DEATH AND BUSINESS I CAN TELL.

THE KING IS MAD: HOW STIFF IS MY VILE SENSE THAT I STAND UP, AND HAVE INGENIOUS FEELING OF MY HUGE SORROWS! BETTER I WERE DISTRACT: SO SHOULD MY THOUGHTS BE SEVERED FROM MY GRIEFS, AND WOES BY WRONG IMAGINATIONS LOSE THE KNOWLEDGE OF THEMSELVES.

GIVE ME YOUR HAND: FAR OFF, METHINKS, I HEAR THE BEATEN DRUM!

COME, FATHER, I'LL BESTOW YOU WITH A FRIEND.

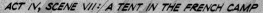

PLEASE YOU, DRAW NEAR.

LOUDER THE MUSIC THERE!

O MY DEAR FATHER! RESTORATION HANG THY MEDICINE ON MY LIPS, AND LET THIS KISS REPAIR THOSE VIOLENT HARMS THAT MY TWO SISTERS HAVE IN THY REVERENCE MADE.

KIND AND DEAR PRINCESS!

HAD YOU NOT BEEN THEIR FATHER, THESE WHITE FLAKES DID CHALLENGE PITY OF THEM.

WAS THIS A FACE TO BE OPPOSED AGAINST THE WARRING WINDS? TO STAND AGAINST THE DEEP DREAD-BOLTED THUNDER? IN THE MOST TERRIBLE AND NIMBLE STROKE OF QUICK CROSS LIGHTNING? TO WATCH — POOR *PERDU!* — WITH THIS THIN HELM?

MINE ENEMY'S DOG, THOUGH HE HAD BIT ME, SHOULD HAVE STOOD THAT NIGHT AGAINST MY FIRE.

AND WAST THOU FAIN, POOR FATHER, TO HOVEL THEE WITH SWINE AND ROGUES FORLORN, IN SHORT AND MUSTY STRAW?

ALACK, ALACK! 'TIS WONDER THAT THY LIFE AND WITS AT ONCE HAD NOT CONCLUDED ALL!

HE WAKES: SPEAK TO HIM!

MADAM, DO YOU: 'TIS FITTEST.

HOW DOES MY ROYAL LORD? HOW FARES YOUR MAJESTY?

YOU DO ME WRONG TO TAKE ME OUT O'TH'GRAVE; THOU ART A SOUL IN BLISS;

BUT I AM BOUND UPON A WHEEL OF FIRE, THAT MINE OWN TEARS DO SCALD LIKE MOLTEN LEAD.

SIR, DO YOU KNOW ME?

YOU ARE A SPIRIT, I KNOW; WHERE DID YOU DIE?

STILL, STILL, FAR WIDE.

HE'S SCARCE AWAKE; LET HIM ALONE AWHILE.

WHERE HAVE I BEEN? — WHERE AM I? — FAIR DAYLIGHT?

I AM MIGHTLY ABUSED. I SHOULD E'EN DIE WITH PITY TO SEE ANOTHER THUS.

I KNOW NOT WHAT TO SAY.

I WILL NOT SWEAR THESE ARE MY HANDS.

LET'S SEE.

I FEEL THIS PIN PRICK.

WOULD I WERE ASSURED OF MY CONDITION!

O LOOK UPON ME, SIR, AND HOLD YOUR HAND IN BENEDICTION O'ER ME!

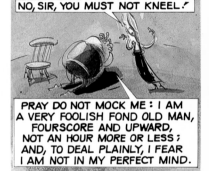

NO, SIR, YOU MUST NOT KNEEL!

PRAY DO NOT MOCK ME: I AM A VERY FOOLISH FOND OLD MAN, FOURSCORE AND UPWARD, NOT AN HOUR MORE OR LESS; AND, TO DEAL PLAINLY, I FEAR I AM NOT IN MY PERFECT MIND.

METHINKS I SHOULD KNOW YOU, AND KNOW THIS MAN;

YET I AM DOUBTFUL:

FOR I AM MAINLY IGNORANT WHAT PLACE THIS IS, AND ALL THE SKILL I HAVE REMEMBERS NOT THESE GARMENTS.

NOR I KNOW NOT WHERE I DID LODGE LAST NIGHT.

DO NOT LAUGH AT ME; FOR, AS I AM A MAN, I THINK THIS LADY TO BE MY CHILD CORDELIA.

AND SO I AM, I AM!

BE YOUR TEARS WET?

YES, FAITH. I PRAY, WEEP NOT: IF YOU HAVE POISON FOR ME, I WILL DRINK IT. I KNOW YOU DO NOT LOVE ME; FOR YOUR SISTERS HAVE, AS I DO REMEMBER, DONE ME WRONG: YOU HAVE SOME CAUSE, THEY HAVE NOT.

NO CAUSE, NO CAUSE!

AM I IN FRANCE?

IN YOUR OWN KINGDOM, SIR

DO NOT ABUSE ME.

BE COMFORTED, GOOD MADAM, THE GREAT RAGE, YOU SEE, IS KILLED IN HIM: AND YET IT IS DANGER TO MAKE HIM EVEN O'ER THE TIME HE HAS LOST. DESIRE HIM TO GO IN; TROUBLE HIM NO MORE 'TILL FURTHER SETTLING.

WILL'T PLEASE YOUR HIGHNESS WALK?

YOU MUST BEAR WITH ME.

PRAY YOU NOW, FORGET AND FORGIVE: I AM OLD AND FOOLISH.

HOLDS IT TRUE, SIR, THAT THE DUKE OF CORNWALL WAS SO SLAIN?

MOST CERTAIN, SIR.

WHO IS CONDUCTOR OF HIS PEOPLE?

AS 'TIS SAID, THE BASTARD SON OF GLOUCESTER.

THEY SAY EDGAR, HIS BANISHED SON, IS WITH THE EARL OF KENT IN GERMANY.

REPORT IS CHANGEABLE. 'TIS TIME TO LOOK ABOUT; THE POWERS OF THE KINGDOM APPROACH APACE.

THE ARBITREMENT IS LIKE TO BE BLOODY. FARE YOU WELL, SIR.

MY POINT AND PERIOD WILL BE THROUGHLY WROUGHT, OR WELL OR ILL, AS THIS DAY'S BATTLE'S FOUGHT.

KNOW OF THE DUKE IF HIS LAST PURPOSE HOLD, OR WHETHER SINCE HE IS ADVISED BY AUGHT TO CHANGE THE COURSE. HE'S FULL OF ALTERATION AND SELF-REPROVING; BRING HIS CONSTANT PLEASURE.

OUR SISTER'S MAN IS CERTAINLY MISCARRIED.

'TIS TO BE DOUBTED, MADAM.

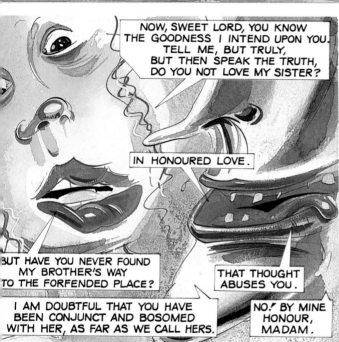

NOW, SWEET LORD, YOU KNOW THE GOODNESS I INTEND UPON YOU. TELL ME, BUT TRULY, BUT THEN SPEAK THE TRUTH, DO YOU NOT LOVE MY SISTER?

IN HONOURED LOVE.

BUT HAVE YOU NEVER FOUND MY BROTHER'S WAY TO THE FORFENDED PLACE?

THAT THOUGHT ABUSES YOU.

I AM DOUBTFUL THAT YOU HAVE BEEN CONJUNCT AND BOSOMED WITH HER, AS FAR AS WE CALL HERS.

NO! BY MINE HONOUR, MADAM.

I NEVER SHALL ENDURE HER! DEAR MY LORD, BE NOT FAMILIAR WITH HER.

FEAR NOT.

SHE, AND THE DUKE HER HUSBAND.

OUR VERY LOVING SISTER, WELL BE-MET.

SIR, THIS I HEARD: THE KING IS COME TO HIS DAUGHTER, WITH OTHERS WHOM THE RIGOUR OF OUR STATE FORCED TO CRY OUT.

I HAD RATHER LOSE THE BATTLE THAN THAT SISTER SHOULD LOOSEN HIM AND ME.

WHERE I COULD NOT BE HONEST I NEVER YET WAS VALIANT: FOR THIS BUSINESS, IT TOUCHES US AS FRANCE INVADES OUR LAND, NOT 'BOLDS THE KING, WITH OTHERS, WHOM, I FEAR, MOST JUST AND HEAVY CAUSES MAKE OPPOSE.

STAY TILL I HAVE READ THE LETTER.

I WAS FORBID IT.

WHEN TIME SHALL SERVE, LET BUT THE HERALD CRY, AND I'LL APPEAR AGAIN.

WHY, FARE THEE WELL:

I WILL O'ERLOOK THY PAPER.

THE ENEMY'S IN VIEW; DRAW UP YOUR POWERS.

HERE IS THE GUESS OF THEIR TRUE STRENGTH AND FORCES BY DILIGENT DISCOVERY;

BUT YOUR HASTE IS NOW URGED ON YOU.

WE WILL GREET THE TIME.

TO BOTH THESE SISTERS HAVE I SWORN MY LOVE; EACH JEALOUS OF THE OTHER, AS THE STUNG ARE OF THE ADDER.

WHICH OF THEM SHALL I TAKE? BOTH? ONE? OR NEITHER? NEITHER CAN BE ENJOYED IF BOTH REMAIN ALIVE.

TO TAKE THE WIDOW EXASPERATES, MAKES MAD HER SISTER GONERIL; AND HARDLY SHALL I CARRY OUT MY SIDE, HER HUSBAND BEING ALIVE.

NOW THEN, WE'LL USE HIS COUNTENANCE FOR THE BATTLE; WHICH BEING DONE, LET HER WHO WOULD BE RID OF HIM DEVISE HIS SPEEDY TAKING OFF.

AS FOR THE MERCY WHICH HE INTENDS TO LEAR AND TO CORDELIA, THE BATTLE DONE, AND THEY WITHIN OUR POWER, SHALL NEVER SEE HIS PARDON;

FOR MY STATE STANDS ON ME TO DEFEND, NOT TO DEBATE.

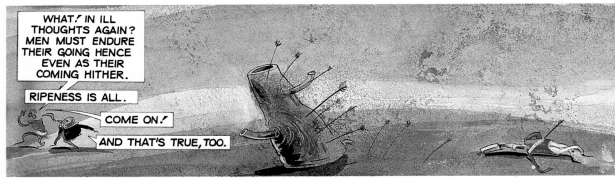

SOME OFFICERS TAKE THEM AWAY! GOOD GUARD, UNTIL THEIR GREATER PLEASURES FIRST BE KNOWN THAT ARE TO CENSURE THEM.

WE ARE NOT THE FIRST WHO, WITH BEST MEANING, HAVE INCURRED THE WORST. FOR THEE, OPPRESSED KING, I AM CAST DOWN; MYSELF COULD ELSE OUT-FROWN FALSE FORTUNE'S FROWN.

SHALL WE NOT SEE THESE DAUGHTERS AND THESE SISTERS?

NO, NO, NO, NO! COME, LET'S AWAY TO PRISON! WE TWO ALONE WILL SING LIKE BIRDS I' TH' CAGE:

WHEN THOU DOST ASK ME BLESSING, I'LL KNEEL DOWN, AND ASK OF THEE FORGIVENESS.

SO WE'LL LIVE, AND PRAY, AND SING, AND TELL OLD TALES, AND LAUGH AT GILDED BUTTERFLIES, AND HEAR POOR ROGUES TALK OF COURT NEWS;

AND WE'LL TALK WITH THEM TOO: WHO LOSES AND WHO WINS, WHO'S IN, WHO'S OUT;

AND TAKE UPON'S THE MYSTERY OF THINGS, AS IF WE WERE GODS' SPIES:

AND WE'LL WEAR OUT, IN A WALLED PRISON, PACKS AND SECTS OF GREAT ONES, THAT EBB AND FLOW BY TH' MOON.

TAKE THEM AWAY!

UPON SUCH SACRIFICES, MY CORDELIA, THE GODS THEMSELVES THROW INCENSE.

HAVE I CAUGHT THEE?

HE THAT PARTS US SHALL BRING A BRAND FROM HEAVEN, AND FIRE US HENCE LIKE FOXES.

WIPE THINE EYES; THE GOOD YEARS SHALL DEVOUR THEM, FLESH AND FELL, ERE THEY SHALL MAKE US WEEP: WE'LL SEE 'EM STARVED FIRST!

COME.

WITH HIM I SENT THE QUEEN: MY REASON ALL THE SAME; AND THEY ARE READY TOMORROW, OR AT FURTHER SPACE, T'APPEAR WHERE YOU SHALL HOLD YOUR SESSION.

AT THIS TIME, WE SWEAT AND BLEED; THE FRIEND HATH LOST HIS FRIEND; AND THE BEST QUARRELS, IN THE HEAT, ARE CURSED BY THOSE THAT FEEL THEIR SHARPNESS.

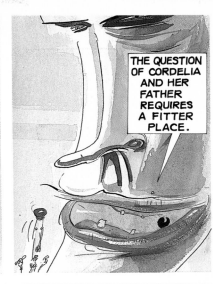

THE QUESTION OF CORDELIA AND HER FATHER REQUIRES A FITTER PLACE.

SIR, BY YOUR PATIENCE, I HOLD YOU BUT A SUBJECT OF THIS WAR, NOT AS A BROTHER!

THAT'S AS WE LIST TO GRACE HIM! METHINKS OUR PLEASURE MIGHT HAVE BEEN DEMANDED, ERE YOU HAD SPOKE SO FAR!

HE LED OUR POWERS, BORE THE COMMISSION OF MY PLACE AND PERSON; THE WHICH IMMEDIACY MAY WELL STAND UP AND CALL ITSELF YOUR BROTHER!

NOT SO HOT! IN HIS OWN GRACE HE DOTH EXALT HIMSELF MORE THAN IN YOUR ADDITION!

IN MY RIGHTS, BY ME INVESTED HE COMPEERS THE BEST.

THAT WERE THE MOST, IF HE SHOULD HUSBAND YOU.

JESTERS DO OFT PROVE PROPHETS.

HOLLA, HOLLA! THAT EYE THAT TOLD YOU SO LOOKED BUT A-SQUINT.

THERE'S MY EXCHANGE!

WHAT IN THE WORLD HE IS THAT NAMES ME TRAITOR, VILLAIN-LIKE, HE LIES!

CALL BY THE TRUMPET: HE THAT DARES APPROACH, ON HIM, ON YOU — WHO NOT? — I WILL MAINTAIN MY TRUTH AND HONOUR FIRMLY.

A HERALD, HO!

TRUST TO THY SINGLE VIRTUE, FOR THY SOLDIERS, ALL LEVIED IN MY NAME, HAVE IN MY NAME TOOK THEIR DISCHARGE.

MY SICKNESS GROWS UPON ME!

SHE IS NOT WELL; CONVEY HER TO MY TENT.

COME HITHER, HERALD, LET THE TRUMPET SOUND, AND READ OUT THIS.

SOUND, TRUMPET!

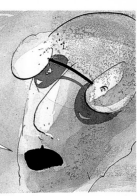

If any man of quality or degree within the lists of the army will maintain upon Edmund, supposed Earl of Gloucester, that he is a manifold traitor, let him appear by the third sound of the trumpet. He is bold in his defence.

SOUND!

AGAIN!

AGAIN!

ASK HIM HIS PURPOSES, WHY HE APPEARS UPON THIS CALL O'TH'TRUMPET.

WHAT ARE YOU? YOUR NAME? YOUR QUALITY?

AND WHY YOU ANSWER THIS PRESENT SUMMONS?

SAVE HIM! SAVE HIM!

THIS IS PRACTICE, GLOUCESTER! BY TH'LAW OF WAR THOU WAST NOT BOUND TO ANSWER AN UNKNOWN OPPOSITE!

THOU ART NOT VANQUISHED, BUT COZENED AND BEGUILED!

SHUT YOUR MOUTH, DAME, OR WITH THIS PAPER SHALL I STOP IT!

THOU WORSE THAN ANY NAME, READ THINE OWN EVIL:

NO TEARING, LADY! I PERCEIVE YOU KNOW IT.

SAY IF I DO: THE LAWS ARE MINE, NOT THINE: WHO CAN ARRAIGN ME FOR IT?

MOST MONSTROUS! O! KNOW'ST THOU THIS PAPER?

ASK ME NOT WHAT I KNOW!

GO AFTER HER!

SHE'S DESPERATE: GOVERN HER!

WHAT YOU HAVE CHARGED ME WITH, THAT HAVE I DONE, AND MORE, MUCH MORE: THE TIME WILL BRING IT OUT; 'TIS PAST, AND SO AM I.

BUT WHAT ART THOU THAT HAST THIS FORTUNE ON ME? IF THOU'RT NOBLE, I DO FORGIVE THEE.

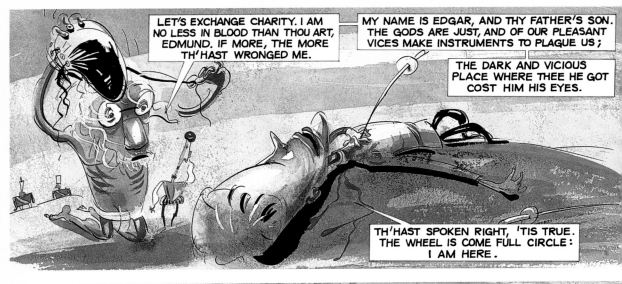

THIS SPEECH OF YOURS HATH MOVED ME, AND SHALL PERCHANCE DO GOOD;

BUT SPEAK YOU ON; YOU LOOK AS YOU HAD SOMETHING MORE TO SAY.

IF THERE BE MORE, MORE WOEFUL, HOLD IT IN; FOR I AM ALMOST READY TO DISSOLVE HEARING OF THIS.

THIS WOULD HAVE SEEMED A PERIOD, TO SUCH AS LOVE NOT SORROW;

BUT ANOTHER, TO AMPLIFY TOO MUCH, WOULD MAKE MUCH MORE, AND TOP EXTREMITY.

WHEN I WAS BIG IN CLAMOUR, CAME THERE IN A MAN, WHO, HAVING SEEN ME IN MY WORST ESTATE, SHUNNED MY ABHORRED SOCIETY;

BUT THEN, FINDING WHO 'TWAS THAT SO ENDURED, WITH HIS STRONG ARMS HE FASTENED ON MY NECK, AND BELLOWED OUT AS HE'D BURST HEAVEN; THREW HIM ON MY FATHER;

TOLD THE MOST PITEOUS TALE OF LEAR AND HIM THAT EVER EAR RECEIVED;

WHICH IN RECOUNTING, HIS GRIEF GREW PUISSANT, AND THE STRINGS OF LIFE BEGAN TO CRACK:

TWICE THEN THE TRUMPETS SOUNDED, AND THERE I LEFT HIM TRANCED.

BUT WHO WAS THIS?

KENT, SIR; THE BANISHED KENT; WHO IN DISGUISE FOLLOWED HIS ENEMY KING, AND DID HIM SERVICE IMPROPER FOR A SLAVE.

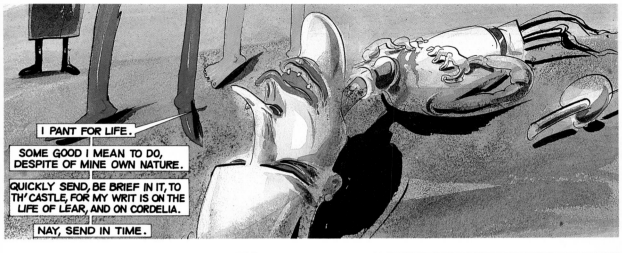

I PANT FOR LIFE.

SOME GOOD I MEAN TO DO, DESPITE OF MINE OWN NATURE.

QUICKLY SEND, BE BRIEF IN IT, TO TH' CASTLE, FOR MY WRIT IS ON THE LIFE OF LEAR, AND ON CORDELIA.

NAY, SEND IN TIME.

RUN, RUN! O RUN!

TO WHO, MY LORD?

WHO HAS THE OFFICE?

SEND THY TOKEN OF REPRIEVE.

WELL THOUGHT ON: TAKE MY SWORD, GIVE IT THE CAPTAIN.

HASTE THEE, FOR THY LIFE!

HE HATH COMMISSION FROM THY WIFE AND ME TO HANG CORDELIA IN THE PRISON,

AND TO LAY THE BLAME UPON HER OWN DESPAIR, THAT SHE FORDID HERSELF.

THE GODS DEFEND HER!

BEAR HIM HENCE AWHILE.

HOWL, HOWL, HOWL! O! YOU ARE MEN OF STONES! HAD I YOUR TONGUES AND EYES, I'D USE THEM SO THAT HEAVEN'S VAULT SHOULD CRACK! SHE'S GONE FOR EVER. I KNOW WHEN ONE IS DEAD, AND WHEN ONE LIVES; SHE'S DEAD AS EARTH. LEND ME A LOOKING-GLASS; IF THAT HER BREATH WILL MIST OR STAIN THE STONE, WHY, THEN SHE LIVES!

IS THIS THE PROMISED END?

OR IMAGE OF THAT HORROR?

FALL AND CEASE.

HE KNOWS NOT WHAT HE SAYS, AND VAIN IT IS THAT WE PRESENT US TO HIM.

VERY BOOTLESS.

EDMUND IS DEAD, MY LORD.

THAT'S BUT A TRIFLE HERE.

YOU LORDS AND NOBLE FRIENDS, KNOW OUR INTENT; WHAT COMFORT TO THIS GREAT DECAY MAY COME SHALL BE APPLIED: FOR US, WE WILL RESIGN, DURING THE LIFE OF THIS OLD MAJESTY, TO HIM OUR ABSOLUTE POWER.

YOU, TO YOUR RIGHTS, WITH BOOT AND SUCH ADDITION AS YOUR HONOURS HAVE MORE THAN MERITED. ALL FRIENDS SHALL TASTE THE WAGES OF THEIR VIRTUE, AND ALL FOES THE CUP OF THEIR DESERVINGS.

O! SEE, SEE!

AND MY POOR FOOL IS HANGED! NO, NO, NO LIFE! WHY SHOULD A DOG, A HORSE, A RAT, HAVE LIFE, AND THOU NO BREATH AT ALL? THOU'LT COME NO MORE. NEVER, NEVER, NEVER, NEVER, NEVER!

PRAY YOU, UNDO THIS BUTTON:

THANK YOU, SIR.

DO YOU SEE THIS?

LOOK ON HER, LOOK, HER LIPS, LOOK THERE, LOOK THERE!